Dr. Abraham Philip l  l
both instruct biblically h
is a unique volume, evidencing the hard w... n
which has resulted in clear biblical truths leading to
appropriate applications. The design of the book around major
biblical themes makes the book a helpful resource for learning key
biblical doctrines and learning how to live in the light of these
doctrines. Dr. Philip's homiletic acumen reveals itself also in
helpful outlines, explanations, and illustrations.

These devotionals are not just presenting a "quick thought for the
day." They are taking us to the Scriptures and to great biblical
truths that by God's grace and through His Spirit will shape our
lives, not just a few moments of our day.

David L. Olford, PhD
President, Olford Ministries International
Memphis, Tennessee

Often in our fast-paced world, many Christians face conflicts that
leave them exhausted and weak. This spiritual warfare is an attempt
by the enemy of our souls to cause Christians to think and, by their
experience, believe that they are carnal, unable to truly represent
the One they serve. Dr. Philip has put together a devotional that
instructs how to grow from strength to strength in dependence on
Christ. This is no ordinary devotional. It reflects the experience of
those who have been in the trenches of struggle and found how to
grow in the Lord.

Daniel E. Lewis D. Min
Administrator
International Association of Grace Ministries
Pinellas Park, Florida

Today, many people are searching for answers to perplexing
questions of life. In *Strength to Strength*, Dr. Abraham Philip presents
divine truths from God's word to help navigate through life and
grow in our faith. I am confident that the Holy Spirit will bless,
change, and strengthen all who read this book.

Rev. Louis Guiliano
Pastoral Care, Hospice Chaplain
Jackson, New Jersey

Dr. Phillip's devotional is truly an inspirational work that strengthens and moves the reader forward in relation to Christ. With his focus on the very real power of encouragement, hope, and growth so resident within the Scriptures, Dr. Philip very adeptly guides the reader through the transformational Biblical truths that identify and address issues at the core of every person. Each daily devotion will immerse you in the truth that sets you free, causes your faith to grow, and empowers you to continue to walk closer and closer toward Christ!

Pastor Christopher Rue
Senior Minister, Word of Life Christian Center
Newark, Delaware


Abraham Philip's life for many years has been based on the eternal truth of God's word. The fruit of this relationship produced *Strength to Strength*. In his book, Dr. Philip plants the necessary seeds for serious Christians to grow spiritually. *Strength to Strength* focuses the Scripture on the great issues of life that confronts everyone in daily living. I highly recommend this book to Christians who want to grow in their faith.

E. E. Elliott, PhD
Department Chair of Biblical Leadership and Ministry
Trinity College of the Bible and Theological Seminary
Newburgh, Indiana


Dr. Abraham Philip has given us a most exceptional work in his book, *Strength to Strength*. By establishing devotional themes centered on historic theological truths such as creation and redemption, Dr. Philip guides his readers into daily adventures of biblical study and personal application. This effort offers substantial scriptural meat, not spiritual fast food. It is for readers who won't be content with the one-verse snack and a quick gulp of commentary. *Strength to Strength* serves us a feast of God's word, both enlightening and challenging us to live daily and abundantly through its transforming power.

Rev. Bruce C. Latshaw
Senior Pastor, The Barn Vineyard Church
Landenberg, Pennsylvania

May the Lord richly bless you
and Empower you to go from
Strength to Strength.

Abraham

Aug, 2018

# Strength
## to
# Strength

# STRENGTH to STRENGTH

*Christ-Centered Devotionals
for
Growing in Faith*

Abraham Philip, PhD

Copyright © 2018 by Abraham Philip

Published in the United States by Proclamation Ministries,
P.O. Box 9700, Newark, Delaware 19714.

All rights reserved. Except as permitted under the U.S. Copyright Act
of 1976, no part of this publication may be reproduced, distributed, or
transmitted in any form or by any means, or stored in a database or
retrieval system without the prior written permission of the author.

Unless otherwise indicated, Scriptures are taken from the Holy Bible,
New King James Version. © 1982 by Thomas Nelson, Inc. Used by
permission. All rights reserved.

Scripture quotations marked NLT are taken from the Holy Bible, New
Living Translation, copyright © 1996, 2004. Used by permission of
Tyndale House Publishers, Wheaton, Illinois 60189. All rights
reserved.

While every effort was made to provide accurate Internet addresses at
the time of publication, the author assumes no responsibility for errors
or for changes that occur after publication.

ISBN-13: 978-1987401608
ISBN-10: 1987401603

# CONTENTS

# Preface

Long ago, King Solomon wrote, "Of making many books there is no end" (Eccl. 12:12). In no genre of biblical literature is this observation truer than in Christian devotionals. Christian devotionals come in many shapes and sizes. There are devotionals for young men and women, older men and women, working mothers, soccer mothers, homemakers, teens, and young adults. In his blog, Whitney Kuniholm of Scripture Union identified devotionals for "early birds, mid-day breakers, commuter-seekers, night watchers, and free spirits."[1] That's not all. There are devotionals for couples, singles, parents, and sports enthusiasts, not to mention holiday and daily devotionals.

Usually, a devotional is 250–350 words long and begins with a personal or human-interest story. The story is then linked to a Bible verse to make a single point and concludes with a question to ponder and a short prayer. By this standard, *Strength to Strength* may not be called a typical devotional, though it may be used as one. Rather, it's a collection of short messages or biblical studies in which the content, structure, and motivational thrust of each message

---

1. W. Kunholm, "What's Your Devotional Type," *The Essential Bible Blog*, http://www.essentialbibleblog.com/2009/07/whats-your-devotional-type.html (accessed June 3, 2015).

are rooted in and governed by the chosen text. They are intended to communicate divine truths drawn from the text and to encourage you, the reader, to grow in the faith. As such, these messages range from 750 to 2,200 words in length and tend to be sermonic in orientation and tone.

The apostle Paul exhorted Timothy, his son in the Lord, who was serving as the bishop of Ephesus: "Till I come, give attention to reading, to exhortation, to doctrine" (1 Tim. 4:13). Paul encouraged Timothy to read God's word privately and publicly, give heed to exhortation, and be grounded in sound doctrine. In a survey of over 5,000 professing Christians, the Barna Research Group found that many respondents showed significant weakness in their doctrinal and theological knowledge. For instance, the survey found that, while most respondents recognized Easter to be a religious holiday, only a minority of adults associated Easter with the resurrection of Jesus Christ. Similarly, many respondents viewed the Holy Spirit as a symbol of God's power or presence but not as a distinct person of Trinity who is equal with the Father and the Son in nature. The Barna Group made this sobering assessment: "As...younger generations...ascend to numerical and positional supremacy in churches across the nation, the data suggest that biblical literacy is likely to decline significantly. The theological free-for-all that is encroaching on Protestant churches nationwide suggests the coming decade will be a time of unparalleled theological diversity and inconsistency."[2]

Mindful of this finding, I assembled into this book thirty-one short messages—one for each day of the month—that I had written over a period of several years. They were originally written for the encouragement of the partners of Proclamation Ministries and collectively relate to five movements of salvation history: creation, alienation,

---

2. Barna Group, "2014," https://www.barna.org/culture-articles/462-six-megathemes-emerge-from-2010 (accessed June 3, 2015).

redemption, sanctification, and glorification. By no means do the exhortations in *Strength to Strength* constitute an exhaustive treatment of these themes, nor are they meant to. Instead, this book is a modest attempt to communicate one or more truths relating to our Christian pilgrimage, which the reader can apply for growing from "strength to strength" (Ps. 84:7). More importantly, these exhortations are about the good news of Jesus Christ—the gospel—and the need for the redemptive ministry of Christ to live what Thomas Kelly describes as a "heaven-directed life...a holy life, transformed and radiant in the glory of God."[3]

I will be the first to admit that there is nothing in this book that you have not heard or read before. Numerous writers and preachers far more gifted than I have published excellent devotionals and books that are of immense help to the body of Christ and continue to illuminate believers who are hungry for God. However, in the words of A. W. Tozer (1897–1963), "if my fire is not large it is yet real, and there may be those who can light their candle at its flame."[4]

This book would not have been possible without the partners of Proclamation Ministries, for they were the initial readers of these exhortations. I am deeply indebted to them, especially the ones who took the time to let me know how much they were encouraged by these messages.

I am profoundly grateful to my friend William Collins for editing the manuscript of this book. A few years ago, we had worked together in the same department during our tenure at the DuPont Company. I thank the Lord for bringing Bill into my path to assist me on this project. His exceptional editing skill for fine-tuning a manuscript while retaining the originality and style of the author is greatly appreciated. His

---

3. T. R. Kelly, *A Testament of Devotion* (New York: Harper & Brothers, 1941), 99.

4. A. W. Tozer, *The Pursuit of God: The Human Thirst for the Divine* (Camp Hill, Pennsylvania: WingSpread Publishers, 1993), 10.

knowledge of the English writers and other literary figures helped me to keep my facts straight. Thanks, too, to all the commentators and Christian authors whose works I have consulted to gain clarity on the theological truths articulated in this book.

I am very thankful to my family for their prayers and constant encouragement. They have been my most valuable critics, saving me from many blunders and mistakes.

Most of all, I thank the Lord who saved me and equipped me to preach the gospel of the kingdom and His love to people in many countries of the world. I owe my utmost to Him who called me out of darkness into His marvelous light. He is my constant companion, my shelter, and my shield. His unfailing love is my succor. To Him belong glory and majesty forever and ever. I humbly dedicate this book to my Lord as an act of worship and adoration.

Abraham Philip
Newark, Delaware

# Introduction

Blessed is the man whose strength is in You,
Whose heart is set on pilgrimage.
As they pass through the Valley of Baca,
They make it a spring;
The rain also covers it with pools.
They go from strength to strength;
Each one appears before God in Zion.

—Psalm 84:5–7

When the great Pharaoh of Egypt asked Jacob, the patriarch, how old he was, Jacob replied, "I have travelled this earth for 130 hard years. But my life has been short compared to the lives of my ancestors" (Gen. 47:9 NLT). Though Jacob had relocated to Goshen, one of the choicest regions of Egypt, with his son Joseph serving as the prime minister of Egypt, he saw himself as a sojourner on earth. He did not see Goshen as his permanent dwelling place. His grandfather Abraham saw himself as a foreigner and visitor among the people of Canaan. The Old Testament heroes of faith did not live to see the coming of the Messiah, but by faith, they saw the fulfillment of the promises of God and "embraced them and confessed that they were strangers and pilgrims on the earth" (Heb. 11:13).

The notion that we are pilgrims on earth traveling to Zion, the city of God, the heavenly Jerusalem, is metaphorically presented in Psalm 84:5–7. The historical background of this beautiful psalm is not precisely known. Some Bible scholars believe that during the reign of Hezekiah, king of Judah, when the Assyrian siege was lifted by divine intervention and the Levites were allowed to enter the temple, they sang this song on their way there (song of ascent). Others suggest that this psalm was composed by David when he was forced to flee from Jerusalem under the threat of Absalom and was prevented from entering the "courts of the Lord." Whatever the historic setting behind its composition, this beautiful psalm aptly foreshadows our pilgrimage toward the city "whose builder and maker is God" (Heb. 11:10).

Our life is a journey. As citizens of heaven, we should not regard the present world as our permanent dwelling place; we are just passing through as sojourners and pilgrims (1 Pet. 2:11). In the first century, Christians were called the "people of the way" and were identified as travelers, making their journey to Jerusalem (Acts 9:2). In the Middle Ages, a Christian was called a *viator*, a Latin word meaning "wayfarer" or "traveler." Anglican theologian John Stott captured this idea succinctly when he wrote, "You are a citizen of heaven, and an alien and exile on earth, a pilgrim traveling to the celestial city."[1] In the annals of biblical literature, no book captures more poignantly the ethos of our pilgrimage than John Bunyan's *Pilgrim's Progress*.

The idea that we are pilgrims on earth does not bode well with many Christians because, while they give a mental assent to the thought that this world is not their permanent dwelling place, they live as though it is and spend their days preoccupied with the here and now. As one writer put it, "Heaven is thrown in as a nice benefit at the end of the ride.

---

1. J. Stott, "The Biblical Basis for Declaring God's Glory," in *Declare His Glory Among the Nations*, ed. D. M. Howard (Downers Grove: Intervarsity Press, 1977), 90.

We want to enjoy life now and cling to it as long as we're able…We don't view ourselves as pilgrims."[2] If the Bible teaches anything at all, it is that we are on a journey of faith toward the New Jerusalem. Only those whose hearts are set on God will reach the finish line. In the text before us, the psalmist draws our attention to three aspects of our pilgrimage.

## A PILGRIM'S STRENGTH

First, we learn of a pilgrim's strength. "Blessed is the man whose strength is in You, whose heart is set on pilgrimage" (Ps. 84:5). Long journeys are not for the weak or faint of heart; they are for those who are strong, resourceful, tenacious, and bold. Just as physical strength is required to make a long journey, we need divine strength to make our spiritual pilgrimage. The psalmist reminds us that a pilgrim whose strength is in the Lord and whose heart is set on pilgrimage will finish the journey.

The Hebrew word `oz, translated as "strength," refers to divine strength bestowed on God's people (Ps. 29:11). Equally important is the idea that God Himself is their strength by which they do what is seemingly impossible (Ps. 28:7–8; 81:1). This word is also figuratively used to describe divine protection. "For You have been a shelter for me, a strong [`oz] tower from the enemy" (Ps. 61:3).

A Christian pilgrim's strength is not an inherent strength, but one that is imparted by God. This is best illustrated by the journey of the Israelites through the wilderness toward the land that God had promised to Abraham and his descendants. After they were delivered from the bondage of Egypt, they were on a journey through a wilderness that was unfamiliar to them. Though the journey was hard and often

---

2. J. S. Cole, "Lesson 10: The Pilgrim Life." https://bible.org/seriespage/lesson-10-pilgrim-life-1-peter-211-12 (accessed May 7, 2015).

discouraging, through it the Israelites discovered God's strength and His faithfulness toward them, whom He had made His own *nachalah* (inheritance).

The Bible says that the Lord led the people by way of the wilderness, equipping them along the way for battle. He went before them by day in a pillar of cloud and by night in a pillar of fire to give them light so that they could travel day and night. When Israelites were terrified by the encroaching army of Egypt and were trapped between the Egyptian army and the Red Sea, Moses encouraged them by saying, "Do not be afraid. Stand still, and see the salvation of the Lord, which He will accomplish for you today…The Lord will fight for you, and you shall hold your peace" (Ex. 14:13–14).

For the first time, God revealed Himself to the Israelites as the "divine warrior" who would fight their battles. He identified Himself as the God of the armies of Israel. Not only that, the angel of God, who went before them as a pillar of fire by night and a pillar of cloud by day, moved behind them to provide a defense against the Egyptians. Thus God demonstrated to the Israelites that He was not only their warrior but also their protector and shelter.

Like the Israelites of old, we too have been delivered from our Egypt (bondage of sin). Jesus Christ, the New Moses of the New Covenant, fought the battle on the cross and delivered us from our bondage. The Bible says, "For this purpose the Son of God was manifested, that He might destroy the works of the devil" (1 John 3:8). Having been set free from our Egypt of sin, we are now on a journey through the wilderness toward our promised land. It is not going to be easy, for we will face barriers and opposition and, at times, experience doubt and restlessness, not to mention rebellion toward God. In these times of testing, we need divine strength to stay on course and be faithful to Him.

When the apostle Paul went through a personal crisis (a thorn in the flesh) that tested his faith, he pleaded with God three times for deliverance. God could have removed the "thorn in the flesh," but He chose not to. Instead, He said to Paul, "My grace is sufficient for you, for My strength is made perfect in weakness." Having been fortified by this promise, the apostle went on to say, "Therefore most gladly I will rather boast in my infirmities, that the power of Christ may rest upon me" (2 Cor. 12:9). He discovered the secret of experiencing divine strength: "For when I am weak, then I am strong" (2 Cor. 12:10). No wonder Paul could say, "I can do all things through Christ who strengthens me" (Phil. 4:13)—not that he could do anything he fancied, but that in Christ he had the strength to be content with whatever state he was in.

God's strength for the journey is inexhaustible. One day, Charles Spurgeon returned home after a hard day's work. He was exhausted and sorely depressed. Suddenly, like a lightning flash, the verse, "My grace is sufficient for you," laid hold of him. After returning home, he pondered on this wonderful promise and quickly realized how absurd it was to disbelieve God in the face of this immutable promise. "It was as though," said Spurgeon, "some little fish, being very thirsty, was troubled about drinking the river dry; and Father Thames said: 'Drink away little fish, my stream is sufficient for thee!'" Simply stated, God's grace is inexhaustible. Cast your bucket in the inexhaustible river of God's grace for strength and help in the hour of need.

We learn from our text that strength for the journey is available to those whose heart is set on pilgrimage. The Revised Standard Version (RSV) translates it as follows: "Blessed are the men whose strength is in thee, in whose heart are the highways to Zion." (Ps. 84:5). "Highway" is a picture of the path of holiness traveled by a Christian pilgrim. The Bible says, "A highway shall be there, and a road, and it shall be called the Highway of Holiness" (Is. 35:8). In Proverbs 16:17, we read: "The highway of the upright is to depart from evil; he who keeps his way preserves his soul."

God who has saved us has also called us with a holy calling according to His purpose and grace that is given to us in Christ Jesus (2 Tim. 1:9). Without the enablement of

Christ, who has called us to holiness, we cannot complete this pilgrimage (John 15:5). Without holiness or consecration unto God, we cannot make this journey and see Him (Heb. 12:14).

## A PILGRIM'S PROGRESS

Second, we learn of a pilgrim's progress. "As they pass through the Valley of Baca, they make it a spring; the rain also covers it with pools. They go from strength to strength" (Ps. 84:6). The expression "strength to strength" points to forward movement toward a predetermined outcome. A Christian pilgrim does not live a static life; instead, he or she is on the move, making steady progress toward the intended destination. C. S. Lewis noted: "Our Father refreshes us on the journey with some pleasant inns, but will not encourage us to mistake them for home."[3] Sadly, many Christians live as though this life is all that matters. They mistake the "pleasant inns" of this life for home and are content with life here and now.

A Christian pilgrim goes from strength to strength. Some translations render it "rampart to rampart" or "army to army." What this suggests is that a Christian pilgrim ought to be characterized by steady growth and maturity. The Bible says, "But the path of the just is like the shining sun, that shines ever brighter unto the perfect day" (Prov. 4:18). Jesus told His disciples that the mark of a person who abides in Him is to bear fruit, more fruit, and much fruit (John 15:2, 5).

The apostle John alluded to different stages in our spiritual growth when he made reference to little children, young men, and fathers in the faith (1 John 2:12–14). Although all who believe in the Lord Jesus Christ, irrespective of their chronological age, are given the right to become the children of God (John 1:12; 1 John 2:13), John maintains that not all are at the same spiritual stage of growth. Some are "children"

---

3. C. S. Lewis, *The Problem of Pain* (New York: HarperCollins Publishers, Inc., 1996), 116.

who have experienced the forgiveness of their sins and fed on "elementary principles of Christ," but do not go on to perfection (Heb. 6:1). If a Christian pilgrim is only content with forgiveness of sins and temporal blessings from God and does not hunger for a deeper knowledge of God, he or she is only a child feeding on milk. "Solid food belongs to those who are of full age, that is, those who by reason of use have their senses exercised to discern both good and evil" (Heb. 5:14).

"Young people" in the Lord are those who are given to the word of God and grow stronger with each passing day (1 John 2:14). They have a history of overcoming the wicked one by faith, which suggests that they are always prepared to fight the good fight of faith wearing the whole armor of God. "Older people" are those who have gone through the preceding two stages and have developed a deeper intimacy with God and know Him experientially. Quaker theologian Richard Foster notes: "It is true that those in the first flush of faith often are given unusual graces of the Spirit, just like a new baby is cuddled and pampered. It is also true that some of the deepest experiences of alienation and separation from God have come to those who have traveled far into the interior realms of faith."[4] Experiencing such hiddenness of God and apparent alienation from God are a part of knowing God.

We are exhorted to grow in all things in Christ Jesus (Eph. 4:5). We are called to grow in the grace of God (2 Pet. 3:18; 2 Tim. 2:1), knowledge of God (Col. 1:10), love for one another (1 Thess. 3:12; 4:10), spiritual discernment (Phil. 1:9), hope (Rom. 15:13), and thanksgiving (2 Cor. 4:15). The apostle Peter echoed the same admonition: "Add to your faith virtue, to virtue knowledge, to knowledge self-control, to self-control perseverance, to perseverance godliness, to

---

4. R J. Foster, *Prayer: Finding the Heart's True Home* (New York: HarperCollinsPublishers, 1992), 19.

godliness brotherly kindness, and to brotherly kindness love…If these things are yours and abound, you will be neither barren nor unfruitful in the knowledge of our Lord Jesus Christ" (2 Pet. 1:5–8).

One of the marks of spiritual maturity is to view the trials of life as divine workmanship conforming us into the image of Christ. The psalmist says, "As they pass through the Valley of Baca, they make it a spring; the rain also covers it with pools" (Ps. 84:6). The Hebrew word *Baca* literally means weeping. No one knows where this valley of *Baca* is located. It's been suggested that the pilgrims traversed through some rough terrain, ravines, and gorges to get to the temple. But when these pilgrims passed through the valley of weeping, they "made it a spring." How could they? A more accurate rendering of the Hebrew text might be, "As they passed through the Valley of Weeping, God provided a spring for them." The Hebrew word *berekah* (pool) means a blessing, divine benediction, or favor. What this suggests is that as the ancient Israelite pilgrims passed through affliction, God turned their affliction into a blessing (Is. 35:7). Similarly, when we pass through difficult experiences in our determination to know God, the Lord turns our "desert experiences" into blessings so that we may know that God's purposes are at work even in our trials.

Where there is no progress, there is regress, and where there is no growth, there is stagnation. In the New Testament, we read about a man named Demas. He is mentioned only three times. In the first instance, Paul introduces him in in his letter to Philemon saying, "Mark, Aristarchus, Demas, Luke, my fellow laborers" (Philem. 1:24). He was regarded equal with Luke and Mark as a fellow worker. It is evident that at this point he was a faithful follower of the Lord.

The second time he is mentioned is in the book of Colossians. Paul now writes: "Luke the beloved physician and Demas greet you" (Col. 4:14). A change seemed to have taken place. Luke is praised as "beloved" and Demas is mentioned only by name. Apparently, he is beginning to slow down. Later, in Paul's letter to Timothy, he writes: "Demas has forsaken me, having loved this present world" (2 Tim. 4:10). In these few words, Paul summarizes the end of a man's life. Demas started out with so much promise but ended in great disappointment. Contrast Demas with Mark. Though Mark was unproductive in his early Christian life, God continued to work in his life and made him extremely useful for the furtherance of the gospel, so much so that he was the first one to write the biography of Jesus Christ.

How do you assess your growth in the Lord? How well are you progressing on your journey of faith? Are you going through a season of dryness in your life? If you are, do not despair. Repent and set your heart on Jesus Christ. Sooner or later, the dry spell will yield to a refreshing rain from above, causing you to mature and become a useful vessel for the glory of God.

## A PILGRIM'S REWARD

Finally, we learn of a pilgrim's reward. At the end of our toilsome pilgrimage, says the psalmist with certainty, "Each one appears before God in Zion." When the ancient Israelite pilgrims reached the temple in Jerusalem, they had arrived at the place designated for meeting with God. Originally, Zion was a Jebusite fortress in Jerusalem, which later was identified with Jerusalem because of its location and was called the city of David. The supreme reward of the Israelite pilgrims was to enter the temple in Jerusalem and appear before God.

But Zion also holds a deeper spiritual meaning. It is identified as the dwelling place of God (Ps. 132:13). The writer of Hebrews encouraged the Hebrew pilgrims saying, "For you have not come to the mountain [Mount Sinai] that may be touched and that burned with fire...But you have come to Mount Zion and to the city of the living God, the heavenly Jerusalem" (Heb. 12:18, 22). Our ultimate reward, then, is to reach the heavenly Jerusalem and see God face to face. Jesus said to His troubled disciples, "Let not your heart be troubled; you believe in God, believe also in Me....I will come again and receive you to Myself; that where I am there you may be also" (John 14:1, 3). In Revelation, we read that the New Jerusalem will descend from heaven and God Himself will be with His people (Rev. 21:2–3), resulting in a grand integration of God's space and ours. Hence we pray, "Thy Kingdom Come."

During our pilgrimage on earth, our knowledge of God is gained indirectly through intermediaries such as creation, revealed word of God, and God's mighty acts in history. This is called "mediate" knowledge. Hence our knowledge of God on this side of heaven will necessarily remain partial. The apostle Paul wrote, "For now we see in a mirror, dimly, but then face to face. Now I know in part, but then I shall know just as I also am known" (1 Cor. 13:12). In this life, our knowledge of God is obscured as though seeing through a thick glass. Hence we know Him only in part.

But when we get to our heavenly Zion, we are graciously granted "immediate" or direct knowledge of God. In this life, we know God by faith; but in heaven, we shall know Him by sight (Job 19:26; Ps. 17:15). The apostle John wrote, "We shall be like Him, for we shall see Him as He is" (1 John 3:2). Catholic and some Reformed theologians call this the beatific vision or the blissful and blessed face-to-face experience with God in which we gain a vision of the essence or inner being of God. We shall have an innate knowledge of God with the greatest certainty. With our mind's eye, we will behold His splendor in all its purity and glory. While we continue to remain as finite beings, whatever we can know about God directly, we will know perfectly.

The requirement for such beatific vision is a pure heart (Matt. 5:8). The writer of Hebrews exhorts: "Pursue peace with all people, and holiness, without which no one will see the Lord" (Heb. 12:14). In view of the glorious reward of seeing the face of Christ, the apostle John wrote, "But we know that when He is revealed, we shall be like Him, for we shall see Him as He is. And everyone who has this hope in

Him purifies himself, just as He is pure" (1 John 3:3). Personal holiness, therefore, ought to be our highest priority as we press onward to Zion.

In his sermon entitled, "The Christian Pilgrim," delivered in 1733, the American theologian Jonathan Edwards said, "Heaven is that place alone where our highest end, and highest good, is to be obtained. God hath made us for himself. 'Of him, and through him, and to him are all things.' Therefore, then do we attain to our highest end, when we are brought to God: but that is by being brought to heaven; for that is God's throne, the place of his special presence."[5] Our reward is to be with God and enjoy Him forever. The apostle Paul considered it an unparalleled gain to be with Christ; therefore, he pressed toward the "goal for the prize of the upward call of God in Christ Jesus" (Phil. 3:14).

Do you regard God to be your highest reward and long to be with Him? Is your heart set on pilgrimage? Is it sprinkled clean with the blood of Christ (Heb. 12:22)? I pray that the Lord will graciously use this little book to kindle in you a deep hunger for God, help you grow from strength to strength in your inner life, and discover that "God is the highest good of the reasonable creature; and the enjoyment of him is the only happiness with which our souls can be satisfied."[6]

---

5. Jonathan. Edwards, *The Christian Pilgrim: The True Christian's Life a Journey Towards Heaven*, ed. H. Rogers and E. Hickman (Seattle: Amazon Digital Services, Inc., 2011), Loc 129.

6. Ibid.

# Creation

Everyone who is called by My name,
Whom I have created for My glory;
I have formed him, yes, I have made him.

—Isaiah 43:7


Posterity will someday laugh at the foolishness of modern
materialistic philosophy. The more I study nature, the
more I am amazed at the Creator.

—Louis Pasteur

# In Search of Significance

Then God said, "Let Us make man in Our image, according to our likeness; let them have dominion over the fish of the sea, over the birds of the air, and over the cattle, over all the earth and over every creeping thing that creeps on the earth."

—Genesis 1:26

What is man that You are mindful of him, and the son of man that You visit him? For You have made him little lower than the angels, and You have crowned him with glory and honor.

—Psalm 8:4–5

One of life's most pressing quests is the search for significance. At one time or the other, we have all asked the questions: Who am I? Where did I come from? Where am I going? In our everyday life, we normally answer "Who am I"? by giving our name. We are identified by the name that is given to us at birth. Dale Carnegie said, "Remember that a man's name is to him the sweetest and most important sound in any language."[1] But the question "Who am I?" is much deeper than a query about our name; it is a quest for our significance. The Dutch theologian Henri Nouwen once said that most of us measure our significance in one of three ways: I am what I do; I am what others say about me, or I am what I have. He quickly pointed out that each of these ways is a disastrous approach to finding our significance. They only give a false sense of significance and lead to disillusionment and emptiness. The kind of work we do, the possessions we have, or what people say about us is not the true measure of our significance. Jesus said, "Take heed and beware of covetousness, for one's life does not consist in the abundance of the things he possesses" (Luke 12:15).

Who does the Bible say we are? From the text before us, we learn that we have no identity or significance apart from our relationship to God. Without God, we merely exist as cosmic orphans. Any significance we might derive from this temporal world is vacuous and as short-lived as the morning mist. In this portion of Scripture, we learn three important truths regarding who we are in relationship to God.

## WE ARE CREATED BY GOD

We learn that we are significant because we are created by God. God said, "Let Us make man in Our image, according to Our likeness" (Gen. 1:26). The psalmist declares that we are made by God. He made us a little lower than *Elohim* (gods). In some translations, it says "angels." Perhaps a better translation is "little lower than divine beings." We are not the product of a cosmic accident or the result of a collision of atoms and molecules in a primordial soup. An atheist who denies the existence of God offers only a materialistic or naturalistic explanation of who we are: in essence, we are a freak accident of nature, with no purpose and meaning to life.

---

1. Dale Carnegie, *How To Win Friends and Influence People* (New York: Simon and Schuster, 1964), 79.

There is no God, no devil, no angels, no afterlife, no meaning and no purpose. Any purpose we may have in life, we create for ourselves. Such a life is hopeless, helpless, and hapless.

But the Bible says we are created by God and for God. You see, God created this universe *ex nihilo* (out of nothing). Having created the universe out of nothing, God created (*bara*) man out of the dust of the earth. He fashioned him in His own image and breathed into him the breath of life so that he became a living soul (Gen. 2:7). Why did God create man? He created man for His own glory (Col. 1:16). God declares, "Everyone who is called by my name, whom I created for my glory...I formed and made" (Is. 43:7).

Notice that God created man in His own image and likeness. What does it mean that we are created in His image and likeness? This does not mean that we are little gods walking around on earth. No, we are mere mortals, and only God is immortal. But we possess to a limited degree some of the attributes of God, such as the power to reason and make choices, the capacity to love and to be kind, to be righteous and holy, and to rule over the earth. The ruling and subduing function of man is an important aspect of being created in the image of God. The fact that we are created in God's image means that we belong to God.

Once, the chief priests and scribes asked Jesus whether or not it was lawful to pay taxes to Caesar. He asked them to show Him a coin. When Jesus was presented with a coin, He asked whose image was on it. They said it was Caesar's. Jesus said render to Caesar what belonged to Caesar and to God what belonged to God. You see, the coin was not Caesar's, but in one sense it belonged to him because his image was on it. So also we who carry the image of God belong to God. We are significant because we are His possession. We derive our significance from our relationship to Him.

But the image of God in us has been shattered by sin, resulting in an identity crisis. This identity crisis is an integral part of our alienation from God. The defaced image of God is unable to reflect the goodness and beauty of God. A pool of clear water is able to reflect the beauty of the shining moon on a summer night. But if we disturb the water by throwing a stone into the pool, or if the pool is churned by a blowing wind, it fails to reflect the full beauty of the moon. The moon is still there, but the broken or disturbed water in the pool cannot reflect the moon's full beauty. We can only see a distorted image. This is the same with the shattered image of God in us. The image is there, but it is ruined. It needs to be restored if it is to reflect the beauty of God. The broken image of God is restored only in Christ because He is the invisible image of God (Col. 1:15).

## WE ARE CROWNED BY GOD

We are significant because we are crowned by God. God made man a little lower than the angels or divine beings. He crowned man with glory and honor. God endowed us with enormous capacities and invested us with the powers to rule that which He created—the fish of the sea, the birds of the air, and the animal on the land. The word "dominion" is a regal term, which in Hebrew and Greek means to rule, to reign, to have authority, to be master. In other words, God appointed man to be the vice-regent or co-regent over God's creation. According to Hebrews 2:8, nothing was excluded from his control. This was the status of man before his fall.

When man rebelled against God and ate of the tree of the knowledge of good and evil, he committed the greatest act of treason, for which the only punishment is death. Thus man became subject to both spiritual and physical death. He became estranged from God. His soul, the seat of his intellect, feelings, and identity, began to die, and man began to lose his sense of identity.

Despite the shattering of the image of God in us, we see evidence of man's rule over God's creation, albeit in a diminished way. The phenomenal discoveries in the last hundred years in earth sciences, planetary sciences, biological sciences, and physical sciences are breathtaking. We have learned to split the atom, decode the human DNA, harness the energy of the sun, explore the solar system, and travel to the moon. Both animals and humans depend on plants for food, but only man is able to plant a garden and cultivate a crop. We have learned to transform deserts into blooming gardens and build skyscrapers on land reclaimed from the ocean. These are just a few examples of man's dominion over God's creation even in our fallen state. Truly, man is crowned with glory and honor.

## WE ARE CHERISHED BY GOD

We are significant because we are cherished by God. The psalmist said, "What is the man that You are mindful of him and the son of man that You visit him?" (Ps. 8:4). A more literal translation of the Hebrew text is: "what is mortal that you are being mindful of him and son of human that you are visiting him." The word "visiting" is from the Hebrew *pawkad*, which conveys the idea of a superior having oversight of an inferior to affect a significant change for better or for worse. In this context, the change is for the better. Before the fall, God visited the man in the cool of the day in the garden. God communed with him. After the fall, the man was thrown out of the garden but was not forgotten. God loved him still. He loved him so much that He visited him again in the person of Jesus Christ.

The Bible says God so loved the world that He gave His only begotten Son. He sent His Son, Jesus, who took the form of man, to display for us what the unmarred image of God looks like in a person. The Bible says that He is the "brightness of His [God] glory and the express image of His person" (Heb. 1:3). If you want to see a perfect man, look to Christ. If you want to see God incarnate, look to Jesus. Jesus is God in flesh. Not only did Jesus come to show what the image of God looks like, but He came so that we may be restored to a right relationship with God and have a new identity as the children of God. We are important because we are the object of God's love and care. Jesus said, "Look at the birds of the air, for they neither sow nor reap nor gather into barns; yet your heavenly Father feeds them. Are you not of more value than they?" (Matt. 6:26).

We don't need to spend our lives searching for our significance, not knowing who we are, where we came from, or where we are going. We are created by God for His glory and purpose. We are crowned by God with glory and honor, but that glory and image of God are marred by sin. The good news is that we are cherished by God. He loves us so much that He sent His son Jesus to restore our lost identity.

Have you made this exciting discovery of knowing Christ and your identity in Him? I invite you to commit your life to Christ. Make Him the center of your life. Martin Luther King, Jr. eloquently said what it means to find our significance in our relationship to God:

> So I say to you, seek God and discover Him and make Him a power in your life. Without Him, all of our efforts turn to ashes and our sunrises into darkest nights. Without Him, life is a meaningless drama with the decisive scenes missing. But with Him we are able to rise from the fatigue of despair to the buoyancy of hope. With Him we are able to rise from the midnight of desperation to the daybreak of joy. St Augustine was right - we were made for God and we will be restless until we find rest in Him.[2]

## PRAYER

*Lord, You created me for Your glory. Help me to recognize this glorious truth and live each day by faith to glorify Your name in all that I do. I thank You for giving me the right to become Your child in Christ. Amen.*

---

2. Beloved Community Project, "Dr. Martin Luther King Jr., Vision, Wisdom, and Teachings," http://belovedcommunityproject.org/vision_king.htm (accessed December 3, 2016).

# God Has a Plan for You

For I know the thoughts that I think toward you, says the Lord, thoughts of peace and not of evil, to give you a future and a hope.

—Jeremiah 29:11

Everyone who is called by My name,
Whom I have created for My glory;
I have formed him, yes, I have made him.

—Isaiah 43:7

Have you ever wondered what God is up to in your life? Did you ever feel that God is on a vacation and is too busy to be bothered by you or concerned about you? If you have, wonder no more. This text should dispel any doubt you may have regarding God's concern for you. The prophet Jeremiah assured the exiles in Babylon that God was mindful of them and had a plan to free them from their captivity. He told them that they would be in captivity for seventy years, after which they would be restored to their homeland.

The message of Jeremiah to the exiles should resonate with us as we live as sojourners and pilgrims in this world.

Yes, in Christ we have been transferred from the kingdom of darkness into the kingdom of light. We have become citizens of the kingdom of God. The golden age to come is realized in principle, but its consummation has not happened yet. In the meantime, we live in this overlap of this present evil age and the age to come called the period of "already and not yet." In this period, we still have to deal with conflicts and tensions, because even though Christ has defeated Satan on the cross, our enemy has not yet been removed from power.

God has not left us alone to fend for ourselves. He has a plan for our lives: a plan for our well-being and not for evil. This should give us the confidence to press forward. We note three truths concerning God's plan for our lives in this text.

## THE COMFORT OF GOD'S PLAN

First, let us take note of the comfort of God's plan. God says, "I know the thoughts that I think toward you." The Hebrew word translated as "thoughts" means plans, devices, or designs that God has for us. It is a matter of great comfort to know that God is thinking of us. We are not cosmic orphans floating in this vast universe with no purpose, direction, or destiny. God is ever mindful of us. The psalmist reflects on the mindfulness of God:

> When I consider Your heavens, the work
> of Your fingers,
> The moon and the stars, which You have ordained,
> What is man that You are mindful of him,
> And the son of man that You visit him? Ps. 8:3–4

> Lord, what is man, that You take
> knowledge of him?
> Or the son of man, that You are mindful
> of him? Ps. 144:3

While God is mindful of all people, it is even more comforting to note that God holds special thoughts and plans toward His covenant people who trust in Him. David wrote:

> Many, O Lord my God, are Your wonderful works
> Which You have done;
> And Your thoughts toward us
> Cannot be recounted to You in order;
> If I would declare and speak of them,
> They are more than can be numbered. Ps. 40:5

God said to Jeremiah, "Before I formed you in the womb I knew you; before you were born I sanctified you; I ordained you a prophet to the nations." (Jer. 1:5). The apostle Paul echoes the same idea when he refers to those who are in Christ as people whom God foreknew (Rom. 8:29). This word "foreknew" points to God's active knowledge of us and His planning. In Eph. 1:4, he calls us chosen in Him before the foundation of the world. Remember Peter? Long before he betrayed Jesus Christ, he was on the mind of Christ. Satan wanted to sift him as wheat, but Jesus prayed for him and interceded on his behalf that his faith should not fail.

Let us take comfort in knowing that we are on the mind of God. The Bible says, "But know that the Lord has set apart for Himself him who is godly; the Lord will hear when I call to Him" (Ps. 4:3). You are special to God. God is mindful of you.

## THE CERTAINTY OF GOD'S PLAN

Second, let us take note of the certainty of God's plan. God says, "I know the thoughts that I have toward you." What God thinks, He will bring them to pass. God does not engage in wasteful thoughts. The Bible says, "There are many plans in a man's heart, nevertheless the Lord's counsel—that will stand" (Prov. 19:21). The psalmist wrote, "The counsel of the Lord stands forever, the plans of His heart to all generations" (Ps. 33:11).

A classic illustration of God's bringing to pass His plans and purposes is found in the book of Genesis. In Chapter 1, we read that God created Adam and Eve and blessed them saying, "Be fruitful and multiply; fill the earth and subdue it;

have dominion over the fish of the sea, over the birds of the air, and over every living things that moves on the earth" (Gen. 1:28). God repeated His intention to Noah and his sons: "Be fruitful and multiply, and fill the earth" (Gen. 9:1).

But when we come to Genesis 11, we discover that people rebelled against God's specific instruction and decided to build a tall tower that could be seen from miles around so that people would not spread over the earth. God was decidedly unhappy about their rebellion and went into action to confuse their language and scatter them to the far corners of the earth. Thus God's plan to fill the earth with people was fulfilled.

We can be assured that God's plan for our lives will come to pass at the appointed time. Though the circumstances of our lives may seem to suggest that God is not concerned about us, we must believe that all things work together to accomplish His plan for our lives (Rom. 8:28). The Bible says, "In Him also we have obtained an inheritance, being predestined according to the purpose of Him who works all things according to the counsel of His will" (Eph. 1:11).

## THE CONTENT OF GOD'S PLAN

Third, let us take note of the content of God's plan. God said, "For I know the thoughts that I think toward you, says the Lord, thoughts of peace and not of evil, to give you a future and a hope." God said to the exiles in Babylon that He had thoughts of *shalom* or peace toward them. God promised the exiles that He would bring them back to their homeland so that they could live in peace and safety and enjoy the covenant blessings. He gave them the promise of hope for the future (Jer. 31:17).

Mathew Henry once said, "Peace is such a precious jewel that I would give anything for it but truth"[1] We all want to

---

1. Sherwood E. Wirt and Kersten Beckstrom, ed., *Topical Encyclopedia of Living Quotations* (Minneapolis: Bethany House Publishers, 1982), 170.

live in peace. We go to distant places, spend vast sums of money, and enter into different relationships looking for peace. But all our efforts seem to bring only momentary peace. True and lasting peace is only found in Jesus Christ, who said, "Peace I leave with you, My peace I give to you; not as the world gives do I give to you. Let not your heart be troubled, neither let it be afraid" (John 14:27). The Bible calls it "peace of God, which surpasses all understanding" (Phil. 4:7). This incomprehensible peace is available to all who put their trust in Jesus Christ, for He is the Prince of Peace (Is. 9:8). Peace is our inheritance, a spiritual blessing in the heavenly places in Christ Jesus (Eph. 1:3).

God promised the exiles that He would bring them back to the Promised Land in order that they would have a bright future, which was their inheritance. The return of the exiles from Babylon to Jerusalem, the city of God, is a picture of an indescribable future that awaits all who are in Christ Jesus. When Jesus told His disciples that He was going to a place where they could not follow Him at that time, they were deeply troubled. They thought they were going to be left without a future. Jesus comforted them with these words:

> Let not your heart be troubled; you believe in God, believe also in Me. In My Father's house are many mansions; if it were not so, I would have told you. I go to prepare a place for you. And if I go and prepare a place for you, I will come again and receive you to Myself; that where I am, there you may be also. John 14:1–3

We have a glorious future in Christ. The Bible describes this glorious future as something that no eye has seen, no ear has heard, and no mind has imagined what God has prepared for those who love Him (Is. 64:4; 1 Cor. 2:9). C. S. Lewis noted that when we are content with mere food, drink, sex, and earthly ambitions, we are like an ignorant child who is content with making mud pies in a slum, because he cannot imagine the pleasure of spending a holiday at the sea.[2] The apostle Paul understood the folly of making mud pies when he said, "For I consider that the sufferings of this present time are not worthy to be compared with the glory which shall be revealed in us" (Rom. 8:18).

Our text also informs us that God wants to bless us with an inimitable hope. The Lord promised the exiles hope for the future, which was theirs if they sought Him earnestly and followed His precepts. But what earthly Israel could not fully possess because of disobedience, Jesus Christ, the true Israel, made possible for us by His active and passive obedience to God. This hope we have through Christ is not some wishful thinking, yearning, or cheery optimism; it is an unshakable trust in the faithfulness of the resurrected Christ to keep His promise of our future with Him. Hence it is called the living hope (1 Pet. 1:3). The Bible calls this living hope "anchor of the soul, both sure and steadfast, and which enters the Presence *behind* the veil" (Heb. 6:19). Only God in Christ can grant us the inimitable hope, which He has promised to us.

How do we appropriate God's promise of peace, future, and hope in our lives as we sojourn in this world? God said through the prophet Jeremiah, "Call upon Me and go and pray to Me, and I will listen to you. And you will seek Me and find Me, when you search for Me with all your heart" (Jer. 29:12). When we pray to the Lord and pursue Him with all our heart, He will hear us, grant our petition, and reveal Himself to us.

## PRAYER

*Dear Lord, thank You for Your promise of peace, future, and hope. Grant me the grace to seek You with all my heart and appropriate Your plan for my life by faith. Amen.*

---

2. C. S. Lewis, *The Weight of Glory* (New York: HarperCollins Publishers, 2009), 26.

## DAY 3

# All for the Glory of God

> Therefore, whether you eat or drink, or whatever you do,
> do all to the glory of God.
>
> — 1 Corinthians 10:31

Each year, on the first Monday of September, we celebrate Labor Day to recognize the contributions of American workers to the social and economic prosperity of our nation. In my view, nowhere in the world is the dignity of labor affirmed and upheld as it is in America. Aristotle regarded some humans as low men consigned to a life of servitude. In the Hindu caste system, the Sudras were relegated to menial jobs and could never aspire to do the work of those belonging to the higher castes. Only in Christianity do we find the dignity of people and their work restored to their rightful place.

Paradoxically, Labor Day is also a vivid reminder that most workers around the world are unhappy with their jobs, since they hate to return to work after a long holiday weekend. For years, job satisfaction has been a major topic of research in psychology and human resources studies.

According to some polls, nearly half of the American workforce is bored with their jobs and many are enormously stressed. Monday is the most dreaded day of the week for many because they have to go to work.

This concern over our attitude toward our work is not simply a matter of academic interest. It has practical implications. The average person spends anywhere from 60%–75% of his or her life in work or work-related activities. How we feel about work affects our health and emotional well-being. One's career is the most important factor influencing the perception of one's "quality of life." It is more important than social life, parenting, money, and even religion. No wonder the famous Scottish writer Thomas Carlyle (1795–1881) said, "Blessed is he who found his work. Let him ask no other blessedness."[1]

Why is there such a high degree of job dissatisfaction? It is because in this fallen world our work has come under the curse of sin so that we can never hope to find ultimate fulfillment or satisfaction in our work, however noble it may be. The Bible says, "All the labor of man is for his mouth, and yet the soul is not satisfied" (Eccl. 6:7). The only way we can find true meaning and purpose in our work is when we do it as an act of worship and a means to display the glory and supremacy of God.

## WE GLORIFY GOD WITH OUR WORK

Why did God put us on the earth? He did so for His own glory. God said through the prophet Isaiah:

> Everyone who is called by My name,
> Whom I have created for My glory;
> I have formed him, yes, I have made him. Is. 43:7

If we are made for God's glory, then everything we are involved in—work, creativity, caring for others, ministries,

---

1. The Quotation Page, http://www.quotationspage.com/ quote/2055.html (accessed December 3, 2016).

relationships, stewardship—should be directed to bring glory to God. In fact, the chief end of our existence is to bring glory to Him.

There is a familiar story about three stonemasons who were building a cathedral. Before long, a stranger walked by and saw one of them carrying rocks from one location to another at the construction site. "What are you doing?" asked the stranger. The mason replied, "Can't you see that I'm carrying rocks?" As the stranger walked by, he saw the second mason at work, so he asked him, "What are you doing?" "Can't you see that I am building a wall," he replied. A few steps away, the stranger came upon a third mason and asked him, "What are you doing?" With great enthusiasm and a smile on his face, he replied, "I'm building a cathedral for the glory of God."[2]

All three masons were at work building the cathedral, but only one regarded his work as glorifying the Lord. The apostle Paul wrote, "Therefore, whether you eat or drink or whatever you do, do all to the glory of God" (1 Cor. 10:31). The dignity of our labor is fully restored and our work becomes a "calling" when we engage in our vocation to glorify God. We cannot hope to find any lasting satisfaction in our work in this sin-tainted world unless we seek the glory of God as the supreme good in our work. This is the only way we can redeem our work from a sense of meaninglessness and purposelessness.

How do you see your work? Do you see it as drudgery, simply a means to earn a paycheck? Or do you see it as an assignment from God to provide for yourself, your family, and those in need? (1 Tim. 5:8–9; Eph. 4:28). Do you see it as an act of worship unto Him? Dorothy Sayers put it well: "Work is natural exercise and function of man...Work is not primarily a thing one does to live, but the thing one lives to

---

2. Howard Butt, Jr., *The High Calling of Our Daily Work: Reflections on Daily Living* (Kerrville, Texas: The HighCalling.org, 2006), 3.

do. It is, or should be, the full expression of the worker's faculties, the thing in which he finds spiritual, mental and bodily satisfaction, and the medium in which he offers himself to God."[3]

I pray that you will consider God's glory your exceeding reward in your work. If you do, you will see your work as a calling from God to serve others and witness for Christ.

## PRAYER

*Dear Lord, thank You for your provisions in my life. Help me to approach my work with the conviction that it is an assignment from You and an act of worship unto You. I offer my work as a service unto You. Amen.*

---

3. Sherwood E. Wirt and Kersten Beckstrom, ed., *Topical Encyclopedia of Living Quotations* (Minneapolis: Bethany House Publishers, 1982), 260.

# Alienation

Therefore, just as through one man sin entered the world, and death through sin, and thus death spread to all men, because all sinned.

—Romans 8:12

Man's sin problem is never cured until his alienation from God is overcome, until the rebellion of the human against the divine is ended, until God and man are brought back together.

—Myron S. Augsburger

# Guilty as Charged

What then? Are we better than they? Not at all. For we
have previously charged both Jews and Greeks that they
are all under sin. As it is written:

"There is none righteous, no, not one;
There is none who understands;
There is none who seeks after God.
They have all turned aside;
They have together become unprofitable;
There is none who does good, no, not one."

—Romans 3:9–12

For all have sinned and fall short of the glory of God.

—Romans 3:23

Woody Allen, who once was married to Mia Farrow,
became estranged from her. During his separation
from her, he began to have a sexually inappropriate
relationship with Mia's twenty-year-old adopted daughter.
When he was asked if what he was doing was right, he said,

"What the heart wants, it wants. There is no logic to it."[1] Jesus said, "For out of the heart proceed evil thoughts, murders, adulteries, fornications, thefts, false witness, blasphemies. These are the things which defile a man" (Matt. 15:19–20). A corrupt heart only wants to do that which is evil.

In the first three chapters of Romans, the apostle Paul establishes that all—Jews and Gentiles—are guilty of sin and stand condemned before God. The Gentile pagan is guilty of not glorifying God, nor thanking Him, in spite of the fact that God has revealed His invisible attributes, eternal power, and deity in nature. Pagans become futile in their thoughts and worship the creation instead of the creator (Rom. 1:18–24). The Gentile moralist is guilty of violating the dictates of his conscience (Rom. 2:14–16). The Jew stands guilty before God for violating His revealed will (Rom. 2:1, 25). The Jew stands just as guilty as the Gentile and deserves God's judgment; the Jew cannot appeal to his covenant relation or Jewishness to be exempt from the judgment of God.

In Romans 3:10–20, Paul, like a skilled coroner, performs a theological autopsy of the natural man and exposes to us the pathology of sin—its vileness, rottenness, and putrefying nature. Why? Unless we see the depth of our ruin, unless we see how lost we are, unless we see how bad we are, we would not appreciate the offer of God's salvation in Christ Jesus. In these verses, Paul describes for us the foulness of man in his fallen condition. Three important truths can be stated about our sinfulness.

## WE ARE UNIVERSALLY SINFUL

First, we are universally sinful. That is, all are estranged from God and have gone their own way. At the fundamental level, sin is not a "thing" or some "force" but a relational construct,

---

1. Walter Isaacson, "The Heart Wants What It Wants," *Time*, August 1992, 61.

a falling away from a good relationship that once existed. Nearly all biblical words referring to sin in the Bible point to this idea: *pasha* (transgression), *chata* (to miss the mark), *shagah* (to go astray), *hamartia* (shortcoming), and *paraptoma* (offense).

This falling away from a relationship with God is called alienation, which is a result of not conforming to the "law of God in act, habit, attitude, outlook, disposition, motivation, and mode of existence."[2] The apostle Paul quotes from the Old Testament: "As it is written, 'there is none righteous, no not one; there is none who understands; there is none who seeks after God. They have all turned aside; they have together become unprofitable; there is none who does good, no, not one'" (Ps. 14:3; 53:3; Rom. 3:10–12). In other words, people avoid God because in their natural fallen state they have no inclination to follow after Him.

What is Paul saying in this passage that is so profoundly diagnostic of the human condition? He is saying that the basic problem with mankind is our alienation from God. Paul uses words such as "righteousness," "understanding," and "seeking" in this text in terms of relationship to God. When Paul says that there is none righteous, he does not mean that there is absolutely no goodness in us, that people are as bad as they possibly can be. Clearly, human experience shows that unconverted people can do good works from a human perspective. Even the drunkard thinks he is better than the thief. But this kind of man-oriented goodness is not what Paul is talking about in Romans 3:10–12. His argument is that in relation to God, from a divine perspective, no one is righteous, no, not one, because even what we perceive to be the noblest deed lacks any saving merit.

## WE ARE HELPLESSLY SINFUL

Second, we are helplessly sinful. When Paul says "no one understands," he does not mean that sin has obliterated our

---

2. J. I. Packer, *Concise Theology* (Carol Stream: Tyndale, 1993), 82.

capacity to reason and that we are devoid of any understanding. Human experience suggests quite the contrary. Many non-Christian scientists and philosophers have made phenomenal contributions to human civilization by their power of reasoning. What's meant here is that sin has darkened our understanding so that we cannot understand spiritual matters without the aid of the Holy Spirit. A person alienated from a relationship with God lacks the capacity and the desire to understand spiritual matters (1 Cor. 2:14).

The crux of Romans 3:10–12 is that sin has alienated us from God. We became unrelated to God and unresponsive to Him due to our broken relationship. Alienation means that man on his own merit cannot find his way back to God unaided by the Spirit of God. The diagnostic term for this condition is "spiritual death." A dead person cannot bring himself to life. He needs to be made alive from the outside. He needs to be regenerated by the Holy Spirit. Jesus said, "No one can come to Me unless the Father who sent Me draws him" (John 6:44).

It is abundantly clear from the testimony of Scriptures that in his unregenerate state, man simply has no desire to seek God. The apostle Paul quotes Psalms 14:2 and 53:1–3: "There is none who seeks after God. They have all turned aside; they have together become unprofitable; there is none who does good, no, not one." The natural inclination of the unregenerate man is not to seek God. He may seek happiness, freedom from guilt, peace of mind, and other benefits that only the true and the living God can give him, but he does not want God. The difference between an unregenerate and a regenerate person is that the former seeks these benefits without the need for God, while the latter seeks these benefits knowing that only in Christ does one finds these blessings and is made complete (Col. 2:10).

What accounts for such a helpless state? It is what Martin Luther calls "the bondage of the will." One of the most important controversies in the history of the church took place in the fourth century. It was a debate between St.

Augustine, the bishop of Hippo, and an Irish monk named Pelagius. The controversy arose as a result of a prayer prayed by Augustine: "Oh God, command us what Thou wouldst. Grant us what Thou commandest."[3]

Pelagius had no problem with the first part of that prayer. Of course, God can command what He wants. He is God. Pelagius' problem was with the second part of the prayer. He said that if God commands us to do something, it means we have the ability to do. It would be unreasonable on the part of God to command us to do something we have no ability to do. Therefore, we don't need any special grace from God to do what He commands us to do. It's nice if He gives it to us, but it is not necessary. He believed Adam's sin only affected Adam, not us. We are sinners because we do sinful deeds by our free will. By the same token, by our will, we can also live without sin.

But Augustine argued that before the fall, man had the ability to sin and the ability not to sin. But after the fall, said Augustine, man's condition changed. He entered into a state wherein he was not able not to sin. In other words, he could not help but sin. So Augustine said that while man has not lost his will or the ability to choose, he has lost the liberty or moral ability to choose God.

The fall did not eradicate our will. We still have the ability to make choices. The natural man makes choices all the time. What we have lost in the fall is the desire for God. And because in our fallen state we are helplessly inclined towards sin, we make sinful choices. As Jesus said, we have turned into a bad tree that only produces bad fruit. This fundamental loss of desire for God is at the heart of original sin. And for that reason, Augustine said God must initiate a work of grace and quicken us or make us alive who are dead in our sins so

---

3. St. Augustine, *The Confessions*, trans. Philip Burton (Toronto: Alfred A. Knopf, 2001), 239.

we can turn to God. God must grant us the ability to do what He commands us to do (John 1:12).

Job lamented, saying, "What is man, that he could be pure? And he who is born of a woman, that he could be righteous?" (Job 15:14). Because sin has corrupted our nature, it is natural for us to desire sin and move towards it. It is like placing a bundle of hay before a lion. The lion has the freedom and ability to eat the hay, but it does not like it or want it, because the lion is a carnivorous animal by nature. Its natural affinity is for meat, not hay. The carnivorous nature drives the lion toward flesh.

## WE ARE RADICALLY SINFUL

In Romans 3:13–18, Paul argues that we are radically sinful. That is, at the core of our being, we all are sinful, and the tentacles of sin have a grip on every aspect of our lives. This is called total depravity. Total depravity does not mean utter depravity. It does not mean a person, without exception, is as bad as he or she can possibly be. What it means is that at the root (*radix* means root) of our being, we are corrupted by sin; therefore, no good work that we can do will earn favor from God for our salvation.

Depravity does not mean that man has no conscience, understanding, or will, but that these faculties are affected by sin such that they cannot be relied on for guidance or salvation. Neither does it mean that people are utterly depraved. Radical depravity means that every aspect of our being has been affected by sin, including our nature, thus rendering us helpless and impotent to save or regenerate ourselves without the aid of the Holy Spirit. The apostle John wrote: "If we say that we have no sin, we deceive ourselves, and the truth is not in us…If we say that we have not sinned, we make Him a liar, and His word is not in us…If we say that we have not sinned, we make Him a liar, and His word is not in us" (1 John 1:8, 10).

In these two verses, John reminds us that we are sinners by nature and by choice. He refers to sin both as a principle working in us and as an act that we commit. In Matthew 5 and 12, Jesus gives the analogy of a good and a bad tree to illustrate the truth that a tree is known by its fruit. Commenting on this passage, Hodge notes:

> The very pith and point of these instructions is that moral acts are a revelation of moral character. They do not constitute it, but simply manifest what it is. The fruit of a tree reveals the nature of the tree. It does not make that nature, but simply proves what it is. So in the case of man, his moral exercises, his thoughts, and feelings, as well as his external acts, are determined by an internal cause.[4]

The Bible paints a grim picture: We are universally sinful. We are helplessly sinful. We are radically sinful. The only way to be freed from the bondage of sin is to experience the sovereign work of grace in our lives. What is lost in Adam is only recovered in Christ, the last Adam. God must make us alive by His work of grace before we can put our faith in Christ. Jesus said: "Therefore I have said to you that no one can come to Me unless it has been granted to him by My Father" (John 6:65).

You need to be drawn by the Father. If you are saved, you should be overwhelmed with gratitude that He drew you unto Himself, not because of anything you have done. Run to Christ and fall at His feet in gratitude for His salvation. If you are not saved and the Father is drawing you by a gentle tug in your heart, run to Christ and fall at His feet and say, "Lord save me, a sinner."

## PRAYER

*Search me, O God, and know my heart; try me, and know my anxieties; see if there is any wicked way in me, and lead me in the way everlasting. Cleanse me with Your precious blood and make me whole. Amen.*

---

4. Charles Hodge, *Systematic Theology*, vol. 2 (Peabody: Hendrickson Publishers, 2008), 241.

## DAY 5

# Celebrating Shame

> Then the eyes of both of them were opened, and they knew that they were naked; and they sewed fig leaves together and made themselves coverings. . . .
>
> The Lord God called to Adam and said to him, "Where are you?"
>
> So he said, "I heard Your voice in the garden, and I was afraid because I was naked; and I hid myself."
>
> — Genesis 3:7, 9–10

Sometime ago, I watched Larry King interview the iconoclastic pop diva Lady Gaga on his show. In the interview, the singer said that she grew up in a Catholic family, believes in Jesus, and prays often. Then she proudly announced: "My show is a celebration of shame!" She went on to explain that her music is all about defying conventional values and codes of morality.

What Lady Gaga said in her interview should not surprise Christians. She was merely echoing the mood of our culture. We live in a society that has its moral compass spinning out of control, where people no longer are ashamed to display

26

their passions, however distasteful and perverted they may be. The Bible warns, "The unjust knows no shame" (Zeph. 3:5).

Interestingly, the history of shame has its beginning in the Garden of Eden, where the first human couple lived. The Bible says, "And they were both naked, the man and his wife, and were not ashamed" (Gen. 2:25). They were not ashamed because they were in a state of moral innocence, for sin had not yet entered into their lives. But the moment they sinned, their moral innocence was gone, their eyes were opened, and they knew they were naked. Their response was not to celebrate their nakedness but to cover themselves with fig leaves. They were ashamed! Thus, shame entered the human experience as a consequence of sin.

## COVERING OUR SHAME

In the Bible, shame represents a state of moral failure in the sight of God. For example, regarding the rebellious people of Judah, God asks: "Are they ashamed of their disgusting actions? Not at all—they don't even know how to blush" (Jer. 6:15 NLT). Paul identifies the enemies of the cross of Christ as those who brag about shameful things (Phil. 3:19). Jude labels false teachers who corrupt the church as "unthinking animals" and "shameless shepherds." Often, the expression "put to shame" is used as an idiom for divine judgment (Ps. 119:31; Dan. 12:2; Rom. 10:11). Indeed, shame has a dark history; it is not something to crow about.

The Bible teaches that when we reject the true God— who has revealed Himself in nature, history, and the person of Jesus Christ—and turn to our own rebellious ways, God gives us up to uncleanness, vile passions, and a debased mind (Rom. 1:24–28). As a result, we end up in a moral pigpen smeared with filth, exchanging the truth for a lie, and worshipping deities of our own making rather than the true God. The apostle Paul writes: "For this reason God gave them up to vile passions. For even their women exchanged the natural use for what is against nature. Likewise also the men, leaving the natural use of the woman, burned in their lust for one another, men with men committing what is shameful, and receiving in themselves the penalty of their error which was due" (Rom. 1:26–27).

Actually celebrating shame is indicative of a debased mind. The Bible teaches that those who practice the works of a debased mind—sexual immorality, wickedness, covetousness, maliciousness, envy, murder, strife, deceit, evil-mindedness, backbiting, boasting, resentment, and hatred—stand to receive the judgment of God (Rom. 1:28–32). The remedy for spiritual nakedness and shame is not celebration, but to be clothed with the garment of salvation (Is. 61:10). Paradoxically, the only place where one can find the garment of salvation is at the cross, the image of shame. For our sake, Jesus Christ endured the cross, disregarding its shame, and died to pay the penalty for our sins (Heb. 12:2). In His infinite wisdom, God turned the cross, the image of shame and alienation, into a symbol of forgiveness, deliverance, and restoration.

For a person clothed with the garment of salvation, shame is a moral deterrent. Paul reminds Christians that it is "shameful even to talk about the things that ungodly people do in secret" (Eph. 5:12 NLT), just as it is shameful for believers to sue each other in a secular court instead of resolving their conflicts among themselves (1 Cor. 6:4–5). Moreover, when we are draped in the garment of salvation, we are not ashamed to preach the gospel of Jesus Christ (Rom. 1:16) or suffer for Christ (1 Pet. 4:16).

As children of God, we don't celebrate shame; rather, we reject all shameful deeds, since God has given us a new way in Christ (2 Cor. 4:1–2).

## PRAYER

*Lord Jesus, empower me to walk in holiness for Your glory. Thank You for redeeming me and sanctifying me for Your purposes. Give me the grace to live a life that brings glory and honor to Your name. Amen.*

# Life Isn't Fair

Behold, these are the ungodly,
Who are always at ease;
They increase in riches.
Surely I have cleansed my heart in vain.
And washed my hands in innocence.
For all day long I have been plagued,
And chastened every morning.

—Psalm 73:12–14

During the presidential election campaigns in 2008, someone asked Senator John McCain why he was behind Barack Obama in the polls. Without missing a beat, McCain replied: "Life isn't fair." Like McCain, we all have felt at one time or another that life is unfair.

The unfairness of life is evident all around us. Life isn't fair when mismanaged corporations are bailed out while the executives of these tanked corporations leave with golden parachutes worth millions of dollars. Life isn't fair for godly people who struggle to make ends meet, while the wicked prosper despite their wickedness. Life isn't fair when the rich get richer and the poor get poorer. It's not fair for the righteous to suffer, experience financial reversals, and be plagued with all kinds of problems, while arrogant, insolent, God-hating fat cats have everything their hearts desire and enjoy a life of ease. Life isn't fair when the righteous suffer from sickness and bodily pain, while the wicked aren't troubled and their bodies are healthy and strong.

One may ask, what's the point in living a "good and a moral" life if it makes no real difference? Read Psalm 73. The psalmist asked the same question: "Did I keep my heart pure for nothing? Did I keep myself innocent for no reason?" (Ps. 73:13 NLT). But the psalmist also concluded: what a difficult task it is to understand why the wicked prosper (Ps. 73:16). We can't make sense of the apparent unfairness of life. It certainly didn't make a whole lot of sense to the psalmist either, until one day he had a meeting with God in the sanctuary.

Now, don't get too comfortable and wallow in your self-pity and put God on trial. The psalmist discovered that outside of a relationship with God, life seems unfair and meaningless. But those who trust in the Lord see God working out His sovereign will even in the midst of the unfairness and injustice that surround us. We learn three lessons from this psalm that are instructive.

## THE FATE OF THE WICKED

First, we learn that the destiny of the wicked is not what it appears to be on the surface—glittery and golden. They are on a slippery slope slouching toward Gomorrah. Their successes, pleasures, and power trips are short-lived. Unless they repent and turn to God, their end is destruction. The Bible says, "There is a way that seems right to a man, but its end is the way of death" (Pro. 16:25). The Psalmist discovered that the life of wicked people is like a dream that is gone when they awake (Ps. 73:20). They are like flowers in a field destined to be blown away by the wind of divine judgment. They will vanish, never to be found.

Friend, if you are frustrated about the apparent successes of the wicked, keep in mind that they are just that—apparent successes. In reality, they live chasing after the wind, without hope, and speeding toward destruction.

## THE DANGER OF BITTERNESS

Second, we learn that a bitter heart distorts our view of God. Embittered and pained by the unfairness of life, the psalmist questioned the justice of God. "I get nothing but trouble all day long; every morning brings me pain," complained the psalmist. He continued, "For I envied the proud when I saw them prosper despite their wickedness." Does this sound familiar to you? How often have we too questioned God and His justice out of the bitterness of our heart?

To question God this way only points to our foolishness, ignorance, and senselessness. If we truly believe that God is God, we can rest easy knowing that He is in control and that "he makes everything work out according to his plan" (Eph. 1:11 NLT). That is quite liberating. On the other hand, if we believe that God is less than what He is, then we feel that He has fallen short and has betrayed us.

## THE GOODNESS OF GOD

Third, we learn that those who belong to God experience His goodness and nearness even in the face of unfairness, injustice, and adversity. How so? He guides, counsels, and leads them to their glorious destiny. Their health may fail, and their spirit may grow weak, but God remains their strength (Ps. 73:26). They will make Him their shelter and speak of His wonderful deeds. Paul wrote, "Therefore we do not lose heart. Even though our outward man is perishing, yet the inward man is being renewed day by day" (2 Cor. 4:16).

Life may be unfair to you in this fallen and sin-tainted world, but God's grace through Christ is sufficient for you to overcome it (2 Cor. 9:12). Just as the psalmist said, you too can say, "Yet I still belong to you; you hold my right hand" (Ps. 73:23 NLT).

One day, Jesus was told that Pilate had killed some Galileans as they were offering sacrifices at the Temple. Pilate may have thought they were rebelling against Rome. "Do you think those Galileans deserved to die because they were worse sinners?" Jesus asked. Surely, it did not seem fair for these Galileans to be killed when they were engaged in a religious ceremony. Jesus said their death had nothing to do with whether or not they were worse than others. Jesus continued: "And what about the eighteen people who died when the tower in Siloam fell on them? Were they the worst sinners?" (Luke 13:1–5 NLT). The anti-Roman Zealots probably thought that these people deserved to die because they had been working for the Romans on an aqueduct project.

But Jesus took the opportunity to use these incidents to make the point that in this fallen world, it is not helpful to talk who is more or less deserving of evil. We all experience evil in some form in this life. One day everyone will die. What is important is to have eternal life that transcends this earthly life. So Jesus said, "I tell you again that unless you repent you will perish too" (Luke 13:5 NLT). Only those who believe in Him will not perish but will have eternal life.

## PRAYER

*Oh God, I come to You with my frustrations, bitterness, and confusion. Forgive my foolish questioning of Your works. Grant me Your peace. I desire You more than anything on earth. Draw me closer to You, and strengthen me to tell others of Your mercies and wonderful deeds. Amen.*

# The Divine Discrimination

> And in that day I will set apart the land of Goshen, in which My people dwell, that no swarms of flies shall be there, in order that you may know that I am the Lord in the midst of the land. I will make a difference between My people and your people. Tomorrow this sign shall be.
>
> —Exodus 8:22–23

Discrimination is forbidden in our culture. None of us likes to be discriminated against in any way. Though the act of discrimination is considered abhorrent in a cultural and social context, it takes on a whole new meaning when we realize that "discrimination" is a weighty but gracious word in God's vocabulary. In the Exodus story regarding the fourth plague of flies, God said to Moses, "But this time I will spare the region of Goshen, where my people live. No flies will be found there. Then you will know that I am the Lord and that I am present even in the heart of your land. I will make a clear distinction between my people and your people" (Ex. 8:22–23 NLT). God doesn't stop there; He repeats two more times His intention to distinguish the Israelites (Ex. 9:4; 11:7).

Why did God favorably discriminate the Israelites from the Egyptians? Certainly, it was not because of any intrinsic merit they possessed. The Israelites were just as sinful before God as the Egyptians. As Adam's children, they stood guilty before a holy God, as did the Egyptians. The answer is found in Exodus 8:23. The Hebrew word translated as "difference" in that verse means "ransom." It literally reads, "And I place ransom (*pedooth*) between people of me and between people of you." God discriminated the Israelites from the Egyptians because they were the object of His sovereign and gracious redemption, which He had promised to Abraham their patriarch several hundred years earlier (Gen. 15:13–16).

## THERE ARE ONLY TWO KINDS OF PEOPLE

From God's point of view, there are only two kinds of people—those who are redeemed by grace and those who are the object of His retribution. The Bible says, "He who believes in Him [Jesus] is not condemned; but he who does not believe is condemned already, because he has not believed in the name of the only begotten Son of God" (John 3:18).

Surely, God shows no partiality based on one's race, color, gender, or station in life, but "in every nation whoever fears Him [Jesus] and works righteousness is accepted by Him" (Acts 10:35). At the end of the day, what really matters is whether or not one is favorably discriminated.

The implications of divine discrimination are enormous. The Bible says, "But know that the Lord has set apart for Himself him who is godly" (Ps. 4:3). The apostle Peter warned: "So you see, the Lord knows how to rescue the godly people from their trials, even while keeping the wicked under punishment until the day of final Judgment" (2 Pet. 2:9 NLT). As redeemed children of God, we can take comfort in the knowledge that God answers our prayers and guards us as He guards the apple of His eye. He hides us in the shadow of His wings (Ps. 17:8; Zech. 2:8). Yes, we may go through fire and flood, but the Lord brings us to a broad place and gives us true fulfillment (Ps. 66:12).

Divine discrimination is not a matter of justice, but of mercy. It is also a matter of God's freedom, for He saves us for His sake and for His glory (Ps. 106:8; Eph. 1:3–14). The fact that God shows mercy on us at all should make us humble. The way to know whether or not we are on the list of God's chosen people is to ask whether or not we are in Christ. If we are in Christ, we are favorably discriminated!

## PRAYER

*Dear Lord, thank You for redeeming me from the slavery of sin and setting me apart for Yourself. Help me to live in a way that brings You pleasure. Guide my steps that I may walk in holiness and in total devotion to You. In Christ's name, I pray. Amen.*

# Redemption

But when the fullness of time had come, God sent forth His Son, born of a woman, born under the law, to redeem those who were under the law that we might receive the adoption as sons.

—Galatians 4:4–5

God creates out of nothing. Wonderful you say. Yes, to be sure, but he does what is still more wonderful: he makes saints out of sinners.

—Søren Kierkegaard

# The Word Became Flesh

And the Word became flesh and dwelt among us, and we beheld His glory, the glory as of the only begotten of the Father, full of grace and truth.

— John 1:14

But when the fullness of the time had come, God sent forth His Son, born of a woman, born under the law, to redeem those who were under the law, that we might receive the adoption as sons.

— Galatians 4:4

Christmas is that time of the year when Christians around the world celebrate the birth of Christ. The apostle John summarized the essence of Christmas in one verse: "And the Word became flesh and dwelt among us, and we beheld His glory, the glory as of the only begotten of the Father, full of grace and truth" (John 1:14). In His mercy, God chose to come down to find us, because in our state of estrangement it is impossible to find Him on our own. God in Christ apprehended us (Phil. 3:12).

Seven hundred years before the birth of Christ, Isaiah prophesied, "For unto us a Child is born, unto us a Son is given" (Is. 9:6). The child Jesus was born, but the eternally begotten Son of God, Christ the Lord, was given to us. Notice how carefully Isaiah chose his words to ensure that no harm is done to the eternality of the Son when expressing the humiliation of Christ in the incarnation.

## JESUS IS GOD INCARNATE

Historic Christianity affirms that when the second person of the Trinity took on the human nature, He did not divest, subvert, deny, or impugn His deity in any way. He remained fully God and fully man at the same time, and when He ascended into heaven, He did not leave His human nature behind. It is forever a part of Him so that the Son of God who is presently seated at the right hand of the Father is Jesus Christ, the God-man. Indeed, the story of the birth of Jesus is the story of divine condescension.

Why did the Son of God take on the human nature? The apostle Paul tells us that He did so to redeem us (Gal. 4:4). The incarnation was necessary for a number of reasons, but the one that is at the top of the list is our redemption. The fourth-century Cappadocian, Gregory of Nazianzus, noted, "For that which he has not taken up he has not saved. He saved that which he joined to his divinity."[1] The author of the book of Hebrews affirmed:

> For it is not possible that the blood of bulls and goats
> could take away sins. Therefore, when He came
> into the world, He said:
>
> 'Sacrifices and offering You
> did not desire,
> But a body You have
> prepared for Me.' Heb. 10:4–5

1. Justo L. Gonzalez, *The Story of Christianity* (Peabody: Prince Press, 2007), 253.

In his book, *Cur Deus Homo* ("why God became man"), Saint Anselm of Canterbury (1033–1109) argued that incarnation was necessary because only one who was both God and man could save us. As man, Jesus was able to die in our place to pay the penalty for our sins; as God, Jesus could make His death infinitely valuable for satisfying the wrath and justice of the Almighty. As stated before, our redemption was the primary reason for the incarnation. Christmas heralds the glorious truth that God in Christ stooped down to lift us when we could not help ourselves. In the incarnation, the infinite moved into the realm of the finite so we may experience the infinite.

The grand message of Christmas is that God in Christ lifted the veil of His hiddenness and entered into our world in flesh and blood to meet us at our point of need. The Bible says, "Behold, the virgin shall be with child, and bear a Son, and they shall call His name Immanuel, which is translated, "God with us" (Matt. 1:23). Christmas heralds the glorious truth that our God is not distant; He is with us.

Seneca, the Roman philosopher, said that our greatest need was for a hand to come down from heaven and lift us up. God has done just that. He let His hand down, as it were, and sent His Son to rescue us. Thank God, He has not left us to fend for ourselves helplessly in this world of sin and strife. He came to lift us and give us hope.

Let the message of Christmas resonate in your heart and strengthen you to face the challenges of your life. Always remember, "The Lord of hosts is with us; / The God of Jacob is our refuge" (Ps. 46:7). The Lord is our Immanuel in whose grip we abide safely. Nothing shall separate us from the love of Christ, and in all things, we shall be more than conquerors through Christ (Rom. 8:35, 37).

## GETTING READY FOR CHRISTMAS

During Christmas, especially when shopping, we often hear the refrain, "Are you ready for Christmas?" We are truly ready for Christmas when Christ who was born in Bethlehem two thousand years ago is born in our hearts. Christmas proclaims the glorious truth that Christ came in fulfillment of the Old Testament prophecies (Rom. 15:8) to reveal God to us (John 1:18), to take away our sins (1 John 3:5), to be an example to us (1 Pet. 2:21), and to transform us (2 Cor. 5:17).

Have you opened your heart to Christ to be born? Have you been born again? Jesus said to Nicodemus, "Most assuredly, I say to you, unless one is born of water and the Spirit, he cannot enter the kingdom of God. That which is born of the flesh is flesh and that which is born of the Spirit is spirit" (John 3:5–6). These wonderful truths should warm your heart as you gather together with your family and friends to celebrate the birth of our Lord.

## PRAYER

*Lord, thank You for coming down to show me the way of life. Though I don't understand the miracle and mystery of the incarnation, I believe, accept, and receive by faith the glorious blessing of Word becoming flesh. Amen.*

## DAY 9

# Infuriating Grace

> Friend, I am doing you no wrong. Did you not agree with me for a denarius? Take what is yours and go your way. I wish to give to this last man the same as to you. Is it not lawful for me to do what I wish with my own things? Or is your eye evil because I am good? So the last will be first, and the first last. For many are called, but few chosen.
>
> —Matthew 20:13–16

I imagine for a moment that you have been working hard for a company for 30 years. After all these years, you attained a level of salary that is worthy of your service. Then you find the company just hired a fresh college graduate at the salary you are making after 30 years of service. Certainly, you are going to be angry because it violates our sense of fairness and justice. We all feel we should be rewarded according to our work.

Even the apostle Peter felt that way. In Chapter 19, he asked Jesus, "See, we have left all and followed you. So what's in it for us?" Peter thought that because of his self-sacrifice in serving Christ he qualified to claim God's favor and eternal life. Jesus was quick to assure Peter that he would be rewarded sufficiently for his service. Then Jesus told a parable to make the point that the kingdom of God operates on a different principle, which actually runs counter to our sensibilities and sense of justice.

In this parable, a rich landowner finds himself in need of workers to work in his vineyard during the harvest season. In those days in Palestine, as is true in many countries today, a rich farmer customarily hired seasonal workers during the harvest to gather the crops before the rainfall. The landowner goes to the marketplace and hires some laborers at 6 a.m. on an agreed wage of one denarius for twelve hours of work. He then goes back to the marketplace at 9 a.m., noon, and 3 p.m. and hires more workers. There was no contract with these workers, just the promise that they would be paid. He then goes to the marketplace again at 5 p.m. and finds some men still looking for work, so he tells them to go to his vineyard and work. He made no contract with them, not even the promise that he would pay them. He just told them to go and work.

When it was time to pay the workers, the landowner instructed his steward or house manager to pay them, beginning from the last to the first. The last ones hired expected one-twelfth of a denarius, but they got a full day's wages—one denarius. You can imagine their amazement. At this point, those who were hired first (the 6 a.m. batch) must have thought that they would get more than what they bargained for since they worked harder than all the rest. But to their horror, they got what they bargained for—one denarius.

The first batch of workers began to complain: "The last men worked only one hour, and you made them equal to us who have labored all day in the heat of the sun." Their complaint was not that they did not get paid. They were upset that the landowner was unjust in paying the same amount of money to those who did not deserve it. They were infuriated by the generosity of the landowner toward those who did not deserve it. In response, the landowner said, "Friend, I haven't been unfair! Didn't you agree to work all day for the usual wages? Take your money and go. I wanted to pay this last worker the same as you. Is it against the law for me to do what I want with my money? Should you be jealous because I am kind to others?" (Matt. 20:13–15 NLT). The story abruptly ends. There is no resolution.

What are we to learn about the kingdom of God from this parable? We learn that eternal life is not inherited by any works we have done. It is the gift of God. We could never lay claim to eternal life by our works of righteousness or personal merit. This is a radically different message, which infuriates all those who seek to earn their salvation by their works. We learn three powerful truths about God's salvation.

## GOD SAVES US SOVEREIGNLY

First, God saves us sovereignly. The landowner said to the complaining workers: Don't I have the right to do what I want to do with my money? A sovereign is one who has supreme power, freedom, and authority over all that he possesses. God is sovereign over His creation. He is also sovereign over history. He is sovereign over our lives. God saves us sovereignly as He wills for His sake and for His own glory. The Bible says, "He works all things according to the council of His will" (Eph. 1:11).

This truth is rigorously sustained by Scripture. God sovereignly chose Israelites out of all the people of the earth to be God's own special treasure (Deut. 7:6). God did not choose them because they were large in number or were righteous or upright. In fact, God said they were a stiff-necked people. Despite all that, God sovereignly chose them for His purpose (Det. 9:4–5, 6–7). He sovereignly chose Isaac and rejected Ishmael. He loved Jacob and rejected Esau even before they were born or had done anything good or bad. This shows that God chooses people according to His own purposes, not according to their good or bad works (Rom. 9:11). God said to Moses, "I will have mercy on whomever I will have mercy, and I will have compassion on whomever I will have compassion" (Rom. 9:15; Ex. 33:19). The apostle Paul reminds us that God sovereignly chose us in Christ before the foundation of the world that we should be holy and blameless before Him (Eph. 1:3–8).

In this parable, the landowner took the initiative to go and hire the workers. The workers themselves could not simply enter the landowner's vineyard and work. They had to be called by the landowner to work in his vineyard. So also, we are called into the kingdom of God. God in Christ took the initiative to come down to save us because we could not save ourselves. The Son of man came to seek and to save that which was lost (Luke 19:10; John 10:16; Ezek. 34:11–12). Salvation is the work of God. God saves whom He wants to save, how He wants to save, where He wants to save, and when He wants to save. Our text says, "Many are called, but few are chosen." Jesus said, "You did not choose Me, but I chose you" (John 15:16).

## GOD SAVES US EQUALLY

Second, God saves us equally. The first group of workers complained, saying, "These last men have worked only one hour, and you made them equal to us who have borne the burden and the heat of the day." The landowner gave equal wages—one denarius—to all workers irrespective of when they were hired. Jesus was teaching a powerful lesson regarding the kingdom of God. In the kingdom of God, eternal life is not dispensed in proportion to one's length of service, personal merit, ethnicity, or station in life. Regardless of who we are and when we enter into the kingdom of God, we are saved completely and equally.

This radical message must have infuriated the Pharisees and Scribes, who believed that they had a special claim to God's favor over the Gentiles by virtue of their righteousness and merit. This parable informs us that eternal life is granted equally to all who are called by God. The thief on the cross, who acknowledged Christ just before he died, was as completely saved as the disciples of Jesus Christ who walked and traveled with Him.

If we were to squeeze a lifetime of 70 years between the waking hours of 7 in the morning and 11 at night, each of us would find ourselves at different times of the day. If you are 20 years old, you would be at 11:34 a.m.; if you are 35 years old, you would be at 3 p.m.; if you are 65 years old, you would be at 9:51 p.m.; and if you are 70 years old, you would be at 11 p.m. At what time of the day are you now in your life? Whatever the time of your life, when you come to Christ by faith, you are saved fully, completely, and equally.

## GOD SAVES US GRACIOUSLY

Third, God saves us graciously. The landowner asked the complaining workers: are you going to be jealous because I am generous? The first batch of workers felt they deserved more pay above what was agreed to because they worked harder than those who came last. Though they received the agreed wages, they were infuriated by the generosity of the landowner toward the workers who did not deserve the wages they got. What the last workers got was the unmerited favor or grace of the landowner.

What is grace? It is God's goodness to those who don't deserve it. Charles Spurgeon and Joseph Parker both had churches in London in the nineteenth century. On one occasion, Parker commented on the poor condition of the children admitted to Spurgeon's orphanage. It was reported to Spurgeon that Parker had criticized the orphanage itself. Spurgeon became very upset and blasted Joseph Parker from the pulpit the following Sunday. The attack was printed in the local newspapers and became the talk of the town.

The next Sunday people flocked to Parker's church to hear what he would say about Spurgeon. When it was time for him to speak, Parker got up and said, "Spurgeon is not in his church this Sunday, and this is the Sunday they use to take an offering for the orphanage. I suggest we take a love offering here instead." The crowd was delighted. The ushers had to empty the collection plates three times. Later that week there was a knock at Parker's study. It was Spurgeon. "Parker, you have practiced grace on me. You have given me not what I deserved; you gave me what I needed."

The workers who were hired last did not deserve to be paid a denarius, but the landowner paid them a denarius out of the goodness of his heart. He knew that they could not feed their families with one-twelfth of a denarius. He showed grace to them. You can imagine how amazed and surprised the undeserved workers were when they got the full day's wages.

God's infuriating grace becomes amazing grace when we recognize that the only wages we are entitled to is death. The Bible says, "For the wages of sin is death, but the gift of God is eternal life in Christ Jesus our Lord" (Rom. 6:23). Our wages is death because we all have sinned. Death is what we are justly entitled to. Eternal life is not our wages or our earnings, but it is a gift that God graciously gives to us. The fact that God even saves us must humble us and cause us to remain grateful to Him. Grace is the great equalizer in the kingdom of God.

God's grace infuriates those who seek salvation by personal merit and works. But this parable teaches us that God saves us sovereignly, for salvation belongs to God. Salvation is not dispensed in proportion to what time in life we enter the kingdom of God. We are saved equally irrespective of our ethnicity, race, gender, or station in life. God saves us graciously.

Salvation by grace is infuriating because it gives no room for taking any credit for our salvation. It says we cannot earn or contribute anything for our salvation, but only stand to benefit everything from it. God's infuriating grace becomes amazing when we recognize that though we are entitled to condemnation, God in Christ saves us for His sake.

And keep in mind that it doesn't matter at what time of the day you enter God's vineyard, the important thing is that you come into God's vineyard in faith. Jesus is calling you to enter into His vineyard. He said, "All that the Father gives Me will come to Me, and the one who comes to Me I will by no means cast out" (John 6:37). Are you willing to respond to His invitation?

## PRAYER

*Dear Lord, thank You for Your gracious work of redemption. By Your sovereign will, You reached out to me and lifted me from my helpless state and made me a citizen of Your kingdom. Help me to walk worthy of Your gospel and live a life pleasing to You. Amen.*

# Christus Has Risen

> But if there is no resurrection of the dead, then Christ is not risen. And if Christ is not risen, then our preaching is empty and your faith is also empty...And if Christ is not risen, your faith is futile; you are still in your sins! Then also those who have fallen asleep in Christ have perished. If in this life only we have hope in Christ, we are of all men the most pitiable.
>
> — 1 Corinthians 15:13–14, 17–19

In 1960, the famous Protestant theologian Paul Tillich visited Japan to meet with some Buddhist scholars. During a conversation with them, he asked: "If some historian should make it probable that a man of the name Gautama never lived, what would be the consequence for Buddhism?"[1] The Buddhist scholars replied by saying that it did not matter if Gautama Buddha lived or not. They added, "According to the doctrine of Buddhism, the *dharma-kaya* [the body of truth]

---

1. "Tillich Encounters Japan," ed. Robert W. Wood, *Japanese Religions* 2 (May 1961): 48–71.

is eternal, and so it does not depend upon the historicity of Gautama." In essence, these Buddhist scholars maintained that the teachings ascribed to Buddha can stand on their own merit even if Buddha had never lived or taught.

This is not the case with Christianity. In his letter to the church at Corinth, the apostle Paul categorically affirmed that the historicity of Christ and His resurrection are the indispensable pillars of the Christian faith. He said that the edifice of Christianity stands or falls with the personage of Jesus Christ and His resurrection. If Christ had not risen, says Paul, our preaching is useless, our faith is in vain, and we have no forgiveness of sin. No wonder that the early apostles preached the resurrection of Christ everywhere they went. The centrality of the apostolic *kerugma* (proclamation) was the resurrection of Christ. In our text, Paul gives three significant implications of the resurrection of Jesus Christ.

## IMPLICATIONS OF CHRIST'S RESURRECTION

First, the resurrection of Christ assures our resurrection. Some Christians in Corinth, living in a culture influenced by pagan and Greek philosophies, doubted the resurrection of the dead. Paul reminded them in no uncertain terms that the resurrection of Christ was a guarantee of their own resurrection. He wrote: "If there is no resurrection of the dead, then Christ is not risen" (1 Cor. 15:13). Our resurrection is inextricably linked to the resurrection of Jesus Christ. Because Christ has conquered death, we can shout in triumph, saying, "Death is swallowed up in victory. O death, where is your victory?" (1 Cor. 15:54 NLT).

A Christian need not fear death. We may fear the process of going through it, but death itself has no power on us. The resurrection of Christ ensures that all who are in Christ will be raised from their graves, and death, the last enemy, will be destroyed. The Bible says, "For if we have been united together in the likeness of His death, certainly we also shall be in the likeness of His resurrection" (Rom. 6:5). We can be confident in our future resurrection from the grave.

Second, the resurrection of Christ attests our faith. The Bible says, "And if Christ is not risen, then our preaching is empty and your faith is also empty" (1 Cor. 15:14). Our faith is not vacuous but is rooted in the living Christ. The resurrection of Christ gives credulity to our message. The gospel message is not something that was developed by the deliberation of a group of people. It is a message centered on the person, death, burial, and the resurrection of Jesus Christ.

The resurrection of Christ also actualizes our justification. "And if Christ is not risen, your faith is futile; you are still in your sins" (1 Cor. 15:17). By His death on the cross, Christ paid the penalty for our sins, but it is by His resurrection from the grave that He made our justification effectual. The Bible says, "It [Righteousness] shall be imputed to us who believe in Him who raised up Jesus our Lord from the dead, who was delivered up because of our offenses, and was raised because of our justification" (Rom. 4:24–25). In Christ, the second Man, we've been made into a new humanity, having been freed from the slavery of sin (1 Cor. 15:45–47).

Because our faith is attested by the resurrection of Jesus Christ, we can preach the gospel boldly, knowing that it is the power of God unto salvation for those who believe. Whenever we preach the death, burial, and resurrection of Jesus Christ, we can expect to see people get saved and their lives changed. Not only that, we have the confidence that we can have victory over sin and live a life pleasing to God by the power of the crucified and risen Christ working in us through the agency of the Holy Spirit.

Third, the resurrection of Christ affirms our hope. The resurrection of Christ gives us hope in a world where it is in short supply. But our hope is not some cheery optimism or wishful thinking. It is a living hope that is rooted in the resurrection of Jesus Christ (1 Pet. 1:3). Our hope is not confined to here and now, but goes beyond the grave. Paul wrote, "If in this life only we have hope in Christ, we are of all men the most pitiable" (1 Cor. 15:19).

Just before the American evangelist D. L. Moody died, he said, "One of these days, you will read in the newspapers that D. L. Moody is dead. Don't believe a word of it, for I will be more alive then than I am now. I will be in the presence of my Lord." During a brief moment of consciousness, he said, "I see the heavens open and the earth receding. I see the faces of the dear children. Oh! This is my triumph. This is my coronation day."[2]

The hope anchored in the resurrection of Christ gives us the confidence to face the storms of life, even death. Because Christ bore our pain and rose triumphantly from the dead, we are motivated to serve as ambassadors of Christ to bring hope and healing to a hurting world.

Do you know this resurrected Christ? If you do not know Jesus Christ as your personal Savior, NOW is the time to make peace with God. Let the living hope that Christ offers rule your heart. I pray that you will enter into a personal relationship with the resurrected Christ and begin a new journey with Him.

## PRAYER

*Dear Lord, help me live each day in the power of the living Christ. Let me know You in the power of Your resurrection so that Christ is magnified in my life. Amen.*

---

2. Wholesome Words, "Echoes from Glory: Selective Sayings," https://www.wholesomewords.org/echoes/moody.html (accessed May 7, 2018).

## DAY 11

# The God Who Forgives

> Then Jesus said, "Father, forgive them, for they do not
> know what they do."
>
> — Luke 23:34

In early spring of each year, Christians around the world remember the death of Jesus Christ and celebrate His resurrection from the dead. Good Friday and Easter are important dates on the Christian calendar, for they hold enormous historical and theological significance to the followers of Christ.

In Luke 23:34, we read the first words spoken by our Lord from the cross as He spilled His atoning blood upon the sand of Golgotha. Jesus interceded for those who were directly involved in crucifying Him, saying, "Father, forgive them, for they do not know what they do." His prayer for their forgiveness was the fulfillment of what the prophet Isaiah foretold seven hundred years before (Is. 53:12). By His prayer and death on the cross, Jesus fulfilled the priestly functions of paying the penalty for our sin, reconciling us to God, and interceding for us (Heb. 9:15; Col. 1:22).

## THE HEART OF THE GOSPEL

God's forgiveness of our sins is the heart of the gospel. The gospel is a message of hope because it says that God has made a provision for us to receive His forgiveness by sending His Son Jesus Christ to die on the cross for our sins. Marghanita Laski, a secular atheist and novelist, while debating a Christian on television, said: "What I envy most about you Christians is your forgiveness. I have nobody to forgive me."[1] But, thank God, there is forgiveness, acceptance, and restoration available to everyone that comes to Christ in faith (Matt 10:32).

What is forgiveness? There are three important Greek words in the New Testament that help us understand the biblical meaning of forgiveness. First is *aphiemi*. This word literally means to let go, remit, or to send away (Matt. 9:2). The second word is *charizomai*, which means to bestow unmerited favor upon an individual. Luke and Paul use this word exclusively in their writings and give it the meaning of forgiveness (Luke 7:42–43; Col. 3:13). Third is *apoluo*, which means to dismiss or release. When we put these three Greek words together, we get the biblical definition of forgiveness. Biblical forgiveness is God's gracious work by which He lets go of the offense we committed against God and releases us from divine retaliation.

It is important to keep in mind that forgiveness does not erase the offense committed against God. Forgiveness does not undo the sin or change history. What forgiveness does is to erase the record of it. The Bible says, "Blessed is the man to whom the Lord does not impute iniquity" (Ps. 32:2). In other words, blessed is the man who is not charged with the offense committed. When Jesus prayed, "Father, forgive them, for they do not know what they do," He was asking God not to charge the Roman soldiers and the Jewish leaders

---

1. John Stott, *Contemporary Christian* (Downers Grove: Intervarsity Press, 1992), 48.

with the specific offense of nailing the Son of God to the cross, for they did not know what they were doing. Stephen, the first martyr of the Christian church, prayed a similar prayer when he was stoned to death. Before giving up his spirit, Stephen cried out with a loud voice, "Lord, do not charge them with this sin" (Acts 7:60).

The Bible teaches that in order to be saved, one must repent, forsake his or her evil ways, accept Jesus Christ as Lord, and believe that God has raised Him from the dead (Is. 55:6–7; Acts 2:38, 3:19, 17:30–31; Rom. 10:9–11, 13). If repentance must occur prior to divine forgiveness, did God answer the prayer of Jesus? How are we to understand Christ's prayer for His enemies who gave no evidence of any repentance at the time of His crucifixion? A closer examination of the text and its historical context shows that Jesus did not pray for their general salvation or for the forgiveness of all their sins. His prayer was very specific. He prayed that they should not be charged with the specific sin of nailing the Son of God to the cross.

In that sense, Christ's prayer for His enemies was answered. But they still needed to repent of their sins and acknowledge Jesus Christ as Lord to be saved. Interestingly, several days later, Peter preached to many of these individuals who were involved in crucifying Christ, and he appealed to them to repent of their sins and turn to God, so that their sins may be wiped away and that they may receive the refreshing Spirit of God (Acts 3:14–20). The Bible says that the priests, the captain of the temple, and the Sadducees were disturbed by the preaching of Peter, but many others who heard the word believed and accepted Jesus Christ as Lord (Acts 4:4). And the church grew from three thousand to five thousand people.

## WE MUST FORGIVE UNCONDITIONALLY

If repentance is the required precondition to receiving divine forgiveness, should we forgive our offenders if they have not asked for our forgiveness? When exercising interpersonal forgiveness in these situations, we should take our cue from Christ's prayer from the cross and graciously (*charizomai*) forgive our offenders even if they have not asked for our forgiveness. Why? We have been forgiven by God freely, and we are never more like Christ than when we forgive.

Have you repented of your sins and accepted the Lord Jesus? Have you received the forgiveness of the Lord? Good Friday and Easter are vital to our faith. Good Friday affirms that Christ paid the penalty for our sin so that God can forgive us of our sins without abrogating His justice. Easter heralds that Christ was raised from the dead because of our justification (Rom. 4:25). His resurrection attests that Christ's righteousness is imputed to everyone that believes. I pray that you will experience God's gracious forgiveness and, in turn, forgive others as Christ instructed us to do (Matt. 18:33–35).

## PRAYER

*Lord Jesus, thank You for forgiving my sins and cleansing my guilty conscience with Your precious blood. Teach me to forgive freely and unconditionally those who have hurt me, even as You have forgiven me freely. Amen.*

## DAY 12

# God of the Second Chance

I called on the Lord in distress;
The Lord answered me and set me in a broad place.

—Psalm 118:5

So I will restore to you the years
that the swarming locust has eaten,
The crawling locust,
The consuming locust,
And the chewing locust,
My great army which I sent among you.

—Joel 2:25

"I am an ex-radio announcer who has fallen on hard times," said fifty-three-year-old Ted Williams, while recounting his sensational and heart-warming story to the world.[1] When his story appeared on the internet, it went viral

---

1. Today, "Homeless man with golden voice: This time I have God," https://www.today.com/news/homeless-man-golden-voice-time-i-have-god-wbna40944077 (accessed May 7, 2018).

almost instantly, generating over three million hits on YouTube. For a decade or so, Ted Williams, a former radio announcer endowed with a velvet voice, had been living on and off the street. "In 1986," said Williams, "I dropped the ball." He got into alcohol and drugs and ruined his career as an announcer and ended up on the streets of Columbus, Ohio—homeless and begging to stay alive. When he was discovered by a newspaper reporter, Ted was living behind some bushes by the side of a freeway. He had hoped that someone would stop and listen to him and give him a chance to use his voice, which he said was a gift of God.

Soon after his story hit the airwaves, offers began to pour in. He got offers from Kraft Foods, the NBA's Cleveland Cavaliers, and other agencies to do voice-over assignments. Now he has a place to live, and most importantly, he got to see his 90-year-old mother in Brooklyn, whom he had not seen for many years.

## GOD ANSWERS OUR PRAYERS

When I heard this story, I was moved to tears of joy. I was reminded of an important truth about God's character: that God is faithful in answering our prayers. We may not always like the answer He gives or His timing, but when God's children call on Him, He will answer. Julia Williams, Ted's mother, said to a reporter: "I've been hurt, my heart is hurt. I prayed and prayed and prayed. And I used to think that maybe God just doesn't want to listen to me." The psalmist says, "I called on the Lord in distress; the Lord answered me and set me in a broad place" (Ps. 118:5). Indeed, God answered Julia's prayer in His appointed time and set her son in a broad place.

Perhaps you may be wondering if God will ever answer the prayers you've been praying for a long time. You may be asking if God will answer your prayer this year. It is not for you to determine God's timing. Your job is to keep the flame of prayer burning. Jesus said, "And so I tell you, keep on asking, and you will receive what you ask for. Keep on seeking, and you will find. Keep on knocking, and the door will be opened to you. For everyone who asks, receives. Everyone who seeks, finds. And to everyone who knocks, the door will be opened" (Luke 11:9–10 NLT). The apostle Paul wrote, "Always be joyful. Never stop praying. Be thankful in all circumstances, for this is God's will for you who belong to Christ" (1 Thess. 5:16–18 NLT). Don't be discouraged. Be persistent in your prayer.

Ted Williams' story also reminds me that God is a God of the second chance. When Dave Kaelin, a DJ with WNCI-FM in Columbus, was asked why this story resonates with people, he answered without missing a beat: "Redemption. Everyone loves to have a second chance." Isn't that the central theme of God's love story in the Bible? God's redemption story teaches us that Christ came into the world to undo the mess the first Adam created and give us a second chance to be reconciled to God. Our heavenly Father's willingness to forgive us and restore us far outweighs our capacity to fail Him. The apostle Peter thought he had irretrievably failed God when he denied the Lord. He thought he had lost his chance to be a fisher of men. So he returned to his old profession.

Imagine how terrible Peter must have felt. His heart must have sunk way down when he went back to fishing. But just when he had lost all hope and was at the end of his rope, Jesus appeared to him. Jesus always appears when we are down and out. Jesus cooked breakfast for Peter, and after they had eaten, He lovingly and tenderly restored Peter and said, "Follow me." Those words must have been music to his ears.

Friend, God is the God of the second chance. As you are reading this devotional, you may be thinking of all the wrong choices you've made in your life, and like Ted, you may be saying to yourself, "I dropped the ball." Don't despair. The Lord says, "I will give you back what you lost to the swarming locusts, the hopping locusts, the stripping locusts, and the cutting locusts" (Joel 2:25 NLT). Here is the good news for you: if you call on the Lord with contrition, He will come to you with healing in His wings (Mal. 4:2). He always will. You can stake your life on His promise.

## PRAYER

*Gracious Lord Jesus, thank You for forgiving my sins. You are able to restore unto us the wasted years of our life, for You are the God of the second chance. Your willingness to forgive and restore is greater than all our failures. Amen.*

# God's Remedy for Suffering

Grace to you and peace from God the Father and our Lord Jesus Christ, who gave Himself for our sins, that He might deliver us from this present evil age, according to the will of our God and Father to whom be glory forever and ever. Amen.

—Galatians 1:3–4

For we do not have a High Priest who cannot sympathize with our weakness, but was in all points tempted as we are, yet without sin. Let us therefore come boldly to the throne of grace, that we may obtain mercy and find grace to help in time of need.

—Hebrews 4:15–16

In his *Dialogues Concerning Natural Reason*, David Hume (1711–1776), the Scottish philosopher and skeptic of the Enlightenment Period (1650–1804), wrote: "Were a stranger to drop on a sudden into this world, I would show him, as a specimen of its ills, a hospital full of diseases, a prison crowded with malefactors and debtors, a field of battle strewed with carcasses, a fleet floundering in the ocean, a nation languishing under tyranny, famine, or pestilence. To turn the gay [merry] side of life to him and give him a notion of its pleasures, whither should I conduct him? To a ball, to an opera, to a court? He might justly think that I was only showing him a diversity of distress and sorrow."[1]

For Hume, the showcase of our earthly existence is the unavoidable distress and sorrow. Like Hume, many people look at our world of suffering and conclude that God does not exist, or if He does, He is either impotent or malevolent. Clearly, suffering is an inescapable reality of human existence. We don't have to look far to find it. The icy sword of suffering looms over us with every breath we take. A former professor of mine used to say, "If you don't think you have problems, just wait. It's in the mail." The Hindu philosophical system begins with the premise that suffering is universal or *sarvam duhkham*. The first Noble Truth taught by Buddhism is that life is suffering. That is, every aspect of life—birth, aging, sickness, sorrow, pain, grief, and death—is suffering. The Bible says, "Yet man is born for trouble, as the sparks fly upward" (Job 5:7).

Why is there pain and suffering in the world? Different belief systems offer different answers to the question of why we experience suffering and pain. To gain a biblical perspective on suffering and God's answer to the problem of evil, we must carefully consider the story of the Bible as it unfolds from Genesis to Revelation.

## REJECTION

The story begins with creation and ends with restoration. Between these two bookends is God's work of redemption. The story begins with the creation of a perfect world with no pain and suffering. Everything that God made—plants, the stars in the sky, sea creatures, birds, animals, and humans—

---

1. David Hume, *Dialogues Concerning Natural Religion*, part 10, (Indianapolis: Bobbs-Merrill, 1947), 196.

was good. God was at the center of this created order, and man had a perfect relationship with Him. Then man rebelled against God. He disobeyed God's commandment and became alienated from Him. Thus, sin entered the human experience and ruined the perfect world that God created for man. Mankind was thrust into a fallen world characterized by decay, disorder, and death. The Bible says, "The wages of sin is death" (Rom. 6:23). As a result, in this fallen world, we all suffer one way or the other, because we all have sinned and come short of the glory of God (Rom. 3:23).

## REDEMPTION

How do we get out of the mess we are in? The answer is redemption. Seneca, the Roman philosopher, cried, "Oh that a hand would come down from heaven and deliver me from my besetting sin."[2] Indeed, God did just that. Two thousand years ago, God sent His Son Jesus Christ to rescue us. The apostle Paul wrote that Christ gave Himself for our sins, that He might deliver us from this present evil age (Gal. 1:4). He loved us and cared enough about our suffering that He came down to become one of us and bear our sin and suffering upon Himself.

The Bible says, "Because God's children are human beings—made of flesh and blood—the Son also became flesh and blood. For only as a human being could he die, and only by dying could he break the power of the devil, who had the power of death. Only in this way could he set free all who have lived their lives as slaves to the fear of dying" (Heb. 2:14–15 NLT).

In His infinite wisdom, God chose the way of suffering (*Via Dolorosa*) to deal with the problem of pain. The angel of the Lord appeared to Joseph in a dream and said, "And she [Mary] will bring forth a Son, and you shall call His name

---

2. Quoted in Erwin Lutzer, *Winning the Inner War: How to Say No to a Stubborn Habit* (Colorado Springs: Victor, 1979), 3.

Jesus, for He will save His people from their sins" (Matt. 1:21). The centerpiece of God's remedy for our suffering is the cross. On that cross, the judgment of God and the love of God met together to lift us from our fallen condition. The psalmist wrote, "Mercy and truth have met together; righteousness and peace have kissed" (Ps. 85:10).

How does God's work of redemption apply to suffering we experience now? While we are in this fallen world, pain and suffering are going to be a part of our experience. However, in Christ, we have a High Priest who sympathizes with our pain and understands what we are going through, so we can boldly approach Him for grace, mercy, and comfort in our suffering. Jesus Christ is Immanuel, "God with us" (Matt. 1:23). In the problems we face in this life, we don't suffer helplessly or fend for ourselves. In Christ, we have all the resources we need to deal with our afflictions and to experience the consolation of God's presence in the midst of our suffering. Even in our pain, we can have our hearts and minds guarded by His peace that passes all human understanding (John 14:27; Phil. 4:6–7). Jesus said, "Peace I leave with you, My peace I give to you; not as the world gives do I give to you. Let not your heart be troubled, neither let it be afraid." (John 14:27).

## RESTORATION

Comfort and peace in the midst of our pain and suffering are a foretaste of the glorious and perfect future that awaits us, which the Bible calls restoration. God's ultimate plan is to restore the created order and usher us into a new heaven and a new earth where there is no more pain, suffering, decay, or death. The Bible describes this state of perfection: "But there shall by no means enter it anything that defiles, or causes an abomination or a lie, but only those who are written in the Lamb's Book of Life" (Rev. 21:27).

Timothy Keller wrote, "The Biblical view of all things is resurrection—not a future that is just a consolation for the life we never had but a restoration of the life you always wanted. This means that every horrible thing that ever happened will not only be undone and repaired but will in some way make the eventual glory and joy even greater"[3]

Perhaps you may be going through a crisis in your life that is causing you much pain and suffering. If so, turn to Jesus Christ, the great High Priest, who understands what you are going through and is able to comfort you with His presence. You may not fully understand the reason why God has permitted this affliction in your life, but you can be sure that He gives you "more grace when your burdens grow greater" and fills your heart with a peace that passes all human understanding. Remember, our pain and suffering here on earth are only momentary, for we have the hope that one day we will be ushered into a new heaven and a new earth where "God will wipe away every tear from their [our] eyes; there shall be no more death, nor sorrow, nor crying. There shall be no more pain, for the former things have passed away" (Rev. 21:4).

## PRAYER

*Dear Lord, thank You for bearing my past, present, and future pain and suffering on the cross. Help me to rest in You, knowing that You are able to bear my burdens, comfort me in my present suffering, and give me the blessed hope of a future when You shall wipe away all my tears. Amen.*

---

3. Timothy Keller, *The Reason for God* (New York: Dutton, 2008), 32.

## DAY 14

# In Remembrance of Me

> The Lord Jesus on the same night in which He was
> betrayed took the bread; and when He had given thanks,
> He broke it and said, "Take, eat; this is My body which is
> broken for you; do this in remembrance of Me."
>
> In the same manner He also took the cup after supper,
> saying, "This cup is the new covenant in My blood. This
> do, as often as you drink it, in remembrance of Me." For
> as often as you eat this bread and drink this cup, you
> proclaim the Lord's death till He comes.
>
> — 1 Corinthians 11:23–26

William Thayer, the nineteenth-century biographer,
wrote, "Gratitude is the memory of the heart...Where
there is no memory of the heart, there is an absence of
grateful feelings."[1] Every year, on Memorial Day, we
remember with grateful feelings our soldiers who sacrificed
their lives for the freedom we enjoy today. We remember the

---

1. William Thayer, *Gaining Favor with God and Man* (San Antonio,
Texas: Mantle Ministries, 1989), 338.

price they paid for our freedom and the blood they spilled on battlefields at home and abroad, including the beaches of Normandy, the swamps and rice paddies of Korea and Vietnam, the desert sands of Iraq, and the mountains of Afghanistan.

To lay down one's life for his or her country is the supreme act of patriotism. A failure to remember such loyalty with gratitude indicates a fundamental defect in our character. The Jewish exiles in Babylon, living in an alien society, lamented, "If I forget you, O Jerusalem, let my right hand forget its skill! If I do not remember you, let my tongue cling to the roof of my mouth" (Ps. 137:5, 6). These were the sentiments of a people who were not only loyal to their country but who also longed for their God.

## THE DIVINE SACRIFICE

Our Lord and Savior Jesus Christ also laid down His life for us. He left the glory of heaven and came down to us for the purpose of laying down His life for our deliverance from the bondage of sin. Before He went to the cross, He instituted the ordinance of the Lord's Supper for us (also called the Lord's Table, Holy Communion, or Eucharist) so that we may remember what He has done for us. Just as Memorial Day beckons us to remember our soldiers with thankfulness, the Lord's Table reminds us of the greatest battle ever fought in human history—the battle for our soul on Calvary's Hill. Two thousand years ago, on a rugged cross, Jesus Christ, God-incarnate, won a decisive victory over Satan, the enemy of our soul, and freed us from the fear of death. The Bible says that He bore our sins and died for us "when we were still without strength...while we were still sinners...when we were enemies" (Rom. 5:5, 8, 10).

Why would God in Christ die such an illogical and irrational death on the cross? In the final scene of the film, *A Beautiful Mind*, we see the brilliant mathematician and economist, John Nash, accepting the Nobel Prize for his work. His journey to the Nobel lectern was a tortuous one, since he suffered from chronic paranoia and severe schizophrenia. As he accepted the Nobel Prize, he asked, "What truly is logic? Who decides reason? My quest has taken me to the physical, the metaphysical, the delusional, and back. I have made the most important discovery of my career—the most important discovery of my life. It is only in the mysterious equation of love that any logic or reason can be found."[2]

There you have it—the logic and the rationality of Christ's death for us on the cross. What seems to us an illogical and irrational death can only be explained by the "mysterious equation" of God's everlasting love for the unlovable. Jesus said, "For God so loved the world that He gave His only begotten Son, that whoever believes in Him should not perish but have everlasting life" (John 3:16). Let us be captivated by God's love that is "greater than any tongue or pen can ever tell."

## THE MEANING OF THE LORD'S TABLE

The Lord's Table is observed in remembrance of Christ's death on the cross. Jesus said, "Take, eat; this is My body which is broken for you; do this in remembrance of Me…This cup is the new covenant in My blood. This do, as often as you drink it, in remembrance of Me" (1 Cor. 11:24–25). Every time we partake of the bread and drink of the cup, we remember with gratitude what Christ has done to reconcile us to God and put us in right standing before Him.

But the Lord's Table is more than a symbol of God's past actions in history; it is also a sign of a glorious present reality—our mystical union with the living Christ conditioned by faith in Him. This spiritual union forms the basis of our

2. The Film Fatale, "Best Film Speeches of All time," http://www.thefilmfatale.me/tagged/A-Beautiful-Mind (accessed April 12, 2018).

communion with Christ and other believers. To be sure, our communion is mediated by the Holy Spirit who dwells in Christ who is the head of the church and in believers who constitute Christ's body. The emblems of the Lord's Supper signify the nourishment we draw from our communion with Christ. Jesus said, "Most assuredly, I say to you, unless you eat the flesh of the Son of Man and drink His blood, you have no life in you" (John 6:53).

The Lord's Table is also a seal that points to our obligation to proclaim the gospel until Christ returns (1 Cor. 11:26). It assures us of God's grace and gives depth and expression to our prayers. The New Testament scholar Tom Wright rightly observed: "The Eucharist is, in a sense, both the highest form of prayer and the first and most basic answer to our prayers. It forms a lens through which all other answers come into focus."[3]

How so? The Eucharist is the highest form of prayer because it invites us to bring to Christ all our hurts, burdens, and needs without fear, knowing that in Christ we have a High Priest who can sympathize with our weaknesses. It is also an answer to our prayer in that it points to Jesus Christ as the one who alone can meet our needs and satisfy us. And as part of that answer, it invites us to come on behalf of others in need and ask God how we might be a part of His answer to their needs.

## PRAYER

*Lord Jesus, You paid a debt that You did not owe and I could not pay by sacrificing Your life for me on the cross. You were broken for my transgressions, and by Your blood, I am cleansed of all my unrighteousness. With a heart of gratitude, I remember what You have done for me. In Christ's name, I pray. Amen.*

---

3. Tom Wright, *The Lord and His Prayer* (London: Triangle, 1996), 46.

# The Church of God

> Now, therefore, you are no longer strangers and
> foreigners, but fellow citizens with the saints and members
> of the household of God, having been built on the
> foundation of the apostles and prophets, Jesus Christ
> Himself being the chief cornerstone, in whom the whole
> building, being fitted together, grows into a holy temple in
> the Lord, in whom you also are being built together for a
> dwelling place of God in the Spirit.
>
> —Ephesians 2:19–22

One of the most significant events in the unfolding of
salvation history is the formation of the church
(*ekklesia*, meaning "called out"). We find the roots of the
church in the covenant God made with Abraham. "I will
bless those who bless you, and I will curse him who curses
you; and in you all the families of the earth shall be blessed"
(Gen. 12:3). Christ is the foundation, the cornerstone, and the
head of the church (1 Cor. 3:11; Eph. 2:20; Col. 1:18). He laid
its foundation by his death and resurrection. The Bible says
that Christ loved the church and gave Himself for her
(Eph. 5:25; 1 Pet. 1:19). Hundreds of years before Christ, the

psalmist wrote concerning Jesus the Messiah, "The stone which the builders rejected has become the chief cornerstone. This was the Lord's doing; it is marvelous in our eyes" (Ps. 118:22–23).

The church as a functioning community of faith came into being after the outpouring of the Holy Spirit on the day of Pentecost (Acts 2:40–42). Theologian Charles Ryrie notes: "Spirit baptism places people in the body of Christ, and since the body of Christ is the church, the church, the body, began when those first individuals were baptized at Pentecost."[1]

While the church is a distinct reality of the New Covenant, it is also continuous with the Old Covenant Israel. The Hebrew word *qhl* is generally translated in the Septuagint (the Greek translation of the Old Testament) by the word *ekklesia*, meaning "called out" ones. It is interesting to note that Stephen, the first martyr of the church, referred to the congregation of Israel in the wilderness as *ekklesia* in Acts 7:38. He said, "This is he who was in the congregation [*ekklesia*] in the wilderness with the Angel who spoke to him on Mount Sinai, and with our fathers, the one who received the living oracles to give to us."

At the time of the dedication of Solomon's temple, 120 Levites gathered together with their trumpets and stringed instruments. When the trumpeters and singers began to praise God in one accord, the house of the Lord was filled with a cloud and the glory of the Lord (2 Chr. 5:12–14). What happened at the dedication of Solomon's temple repeated itself on the day of Pentecost, when the Holy Spirit came down as a rushing wind and filled the whole house where 120 were gathered in one accord (Acts 1:15; 2:1–4).

God "called out" Abraham to make a great nation—Israel—that would follow after God. He bore the Israelites on "eagles' wings" and called them his "peculiar treasure"

---

1. Charles Ryrie, *Basic Theology* (Chicago: Moody Publishers, 1986), 466.

(Ex. 19:4–5). They were to walk in His ways and be a kingdom of priests and a holy nation (Ex. 10:6). But earthly Israel failed to live up to God's expectation. The Israelites drifted away from God to the point where God said, "You are not my people" (Hos. 1:9–10). But God did not abandon His plan to carve out a people for Himself. He would accomplish His grand purpose through His Son, Jesus Christ, the true Israel whom He called out of Egypt (Matt. 2:15).

Jesus succeeded where earthly Israel failed, for He lived in absolute obedience to the will of His Father in heaven. He fulfilled the demands of the law by His active obedience and died on the cross for our sins. Having risen from the grave, He became the firstborn among many brethren (Rom. 8:29). Thus Jesus Christ made the way for both Jews and Gentiles to be united into a new humanity through faith in Him. This new humanity is the church of God. The apostle Peter calls this new humanity "a chosen generation, a royal priesthood, a holy nation, His own special people" (1 Pet. 2:9).

The New Covenant church is discontinuous with Israel in that all the rituals, sacrifices, and ceremonial laws are no longer binding on the church because of the finished work of Christ. Our status as the children of God is not based on our keeping the laws and ceremonies of the Old Covenant, but on faith in Jesus Christ. Paul wrote, "Therefore know that only those who are of faith are sons of Abraham" (Gal. 3: 7). Membership to the covenant community is no longer limited to ethnic Jews but is open to all who are redeemed by the blood of Christ (Eph. 2–3; Rev. 5: 9–10). The Holy Spirit is poured out on all flesh (democratization of the Spirit), so that every person born of the Spirit has fellowship with Christ (Joel 2:28–32; Acts 2:17–21; 1 John 1:3), receives ministry from Christ (John 12:32; Eph. 2:17), and is identified as belonging to Christ by the seal of the Holy Spirit (2 Cor. 1:22).

In our text (Eph. 2:19–22), the apostle Paul uses three metaphors—kingdom, household, and temple—to describe the church. As people of God, says Paul, we are citizens of a new kingdom—the kingdom of God. We are in this world, but not of this world (John 17:16), for our citizenship is in heaven (Phil. 3:20). Not only that, we are the household of God. That is, irrespective of our nationality, race, ethnicity, gender, or station in life, we are members of the family of God, related to each other by our union with Christ. We are also the temple of God. Under the Old Covenant, people went to a physical temple in Jerusalem to meet with God, but under the New Covenant, we take the temple of God wherever we go, because we are God's temple and the dwelling place of His Spirit. Christ is the cornerstone of this temple; His teachings, as transmitted to us by the apostles, are its foundation; and we are the building blocks fitted together to form a holy sanctuary unto God.

## THE CHURCH IS CATHOLIC

What are the key attributes of the New Covenant church? First, we learn that the New Covenant church is catholic. The word "catholic" means universal. The church is catholic because it is worldwide in extent. The Old Covenant was exclusive to Israel, but under the New Covenant, Jews and Gentiles are brought together as one body in Christ (Eph. 2:14). In his letter to the church at Smyrna, second-century church father Ignatius, wrote, "Where the bishop is to be seen, there let all his people be; just as wherever Jesus Christ is present, we have the world-wide [catholic] Church."[2]

The New Covenant church includes all believers from every corner of the world, without distinction of race, ethnicity, culture, language or gender. "Now, therefore, you are no longer strangers and foreigners, but fellow citizens with the saints" (Eph. 2:19). Beginning in the third century, however, the term "catholic" was used in a polemic sense to distinguish the Orthodox Church from heretical groups.

---

2. The Apostolic Fathers, *Early Christian Writings*, trans. Maxwell Staniforth (New York: Dorset Press, 1968), 121.

## THE CHURCH IS APOSTOLIC

Second, the New Covenant church is apostolic because it is founded on apostolic teachings. The Jerusalem church was apostolic, not because the apostles were in their midst, but because they "continued steadfastly in the apostles' doctrine (Acts 2:42). The church is apostolic because it accepted the teaching of the apostles as canonical.

To claim that the church is apostolic is not to assert that there is a line of succession through any individual. Instead, it is to recognize that the message of the apostles, as mediated through Scripture, is the message of the church. Moreover, the church is apostolic in the sense that it exists in the world with a mission—to spread the gospel. Just as the apostles were sent to preach the gospel, the church exists to take the gospel to the entire world.

## THE CHURCH IS ONE

Third, the New Covenant church is one. It is made of people who are "fitted together" and "built together" for a dwelling place of God in the Spirit. From God's perspective, there is only one church, which is made up of people who are called by the sovereign grace of God and redeemed by the blood of Jesus Christ. The Bible calls these "called out" ones the elect of God (Col. 3:12; 1 Pet. 1:2). Moreover, the church of God consists of the redeemed who are physically dead (church triumphant) and who are physically alive (church militant).

It is important to keep in mind that the true church of God is invisible to us in the sense that only God knows which people among those who attend local churches and profess to be Christians are truly regenerated by the Holy Spirit and living in fellowship with Christ (2 Tim. 2:19). Jesus warned: "Not everyone who says to Me, 'Lord, Lord,' shall enter the kingdom of heaven, but he who does the will of My Father in heaven" (Matt. 7:21).

The distinction between the visible and the invisible church of God is drawn not to say that there are two churches, but to highlight the fact that not all who attend visible local churches are necessarily members of the true church of God. The Bible says: "Examine yourselves as to whether you are in the faith. Test yourselves. Do you not know yourselves, that Jesus Christ is in you?—unless indeed you are disqualified" (2 Cor. 13:5).

The unity of the church is spiritual in nature. The basis of our unity with each other is our mystical union with Christ (1 Cor. 12:13). The apostle Paul reminds us that there is neither Jew nor Greek, slave nor free, male nor female: we are all one in Christ (Gal. 3:28). Unity does not mean uniformity. The Bible teaches that there are diversities of gifts, but the same Spirit; differences of ministries, but the same Lord; diversities of activities, but the same God (1 Cor. 12:4–6). Even in the early apostolic days, there was no uniformity among the churches in their composition, gifts, or mode of worship. Uniformity and institutional unity are not prerequisites for spiritual unity, but genuine spiritual unity finds its expression visibly in institutional unity.

## THE CHURCH IS HOLY

Fourth, the New Covenant church is holy. We learn from our text that the redeemed people of God are fitted together to grow into a holy temple in the Lord. The church is holy in the sense that it is separated from the world and is set apart unto God. This is the church's positional holiness. That's why the church is called the congregation and communion of saints.

At the same time, the church is also progressively being made holy in its inner life (Heb. 10:14), which inevitably finds expression on the outside (1 Pet. 1:15–16). In Ephesians 5:25–27, the apostle Paul calls the church the bride of Christ and says that Christ gave Himself for the church that He might sanctify her, that He might present her to Himself as His glorious bride, without spot or wrinkle. Regarding the holiness of the church, John Calvin noted:

Yet it also is no less true that the Lord is daily at work in smoothing out wrinkles and cleansing spots. From this, it follows that the church's holiness is not yet complete. The church is holy, then, in the sense that it is daily advancing and is not yet perfect; it makes progress from day to day but has not yet reached its goal of holiness.[3]

Our text ends with a solemn reminder that the church of God is a holy temple made of redeemed people who are fitted and built together for a dwelling place of God in the Spirit. Under the Old Covenant, the temple in Jerusalem was the center of worship and national life of Israel. Worship in the temple involved blood sacrifices of animals, prayers, and priestly intercession. Jesus called the temple the "house of God" (Matt. 12:4) and the "house of prayer" (Mark 11:17). He taught that the church is the New Covenant temple of God (Matt. 16:18) and that He dwells among His people (Matt. 18:19–20; John 14:23).

The central activity of the church, which is the gathering of God's people, ought to be worship. Because Jesus Christ offered Himself once and for all when He died for us, we no longer offer blood sacrifices (Heb. 7:27). Instead, we offer the sacrifice of praise and thanksgiving, which is the fruit of our lips (Heb. 13:15). The apostle Peter wrote, "You also, as living stones, are being built up a spiritual house, a holy priesthood, to offer up spiritual sacrifices acceptable to God through Jesus Christ" (1 Pet. 2:5).

The key elements of corporate worship in the church are preaching of God's word, fellowship, partaking in the Lord's Supper, and offering of prayers (Acts 2:42). In addition, people are free to express their joy in the Lord through the singing of psalms, hymns, and spiritual songs (Eph. 5:19). The church, indeed, is the creation of God. The Bible calls it

---

3. John Calvin, *Institutes of the Christian Religion*, ed. John T. McNeil, trans. Ford Lewis Battles (Louisville: Westminster John Knox, 2006), 2:1031.

the body of Christ (Rom. 12; 1 Cor. 1:2; Eph. 4:15). As such, we should never forsake assembling with God's people for the purpose of fellowship, worship, and exhortation (Heb. 10:25). Cyprian of Carthage, a third-century church father, captured the centrality of the church in the life of a believer in these inimitable words: "No one can have God for a Father who no longer has the church for a mother."[4]

## PRAYER

*Lord, thank You for redeeming me and making me a member of Your family. Help me to be a living sanctuary of praise and worship. Empower me to worship You in spirit and truth. Amen.*

---

4. Stephen Tomkins, *A Short History of Christianity* (Grand Rapids: William B. Eerdmans Publishing Company, 2005), 41.

# Sanctification

But in a great house there are not only vessels of gold and silver, but also of wood and clay, some for honor and some for dishonor. Therefore if anyone cleanses himself from the latter, he will be a vessel for honor, sanctified and useful for the Master, prepared for every good work.

—2 Tim. 2:20–21

Sanctification means being made one with Jesus so that the disposition that ruled Him will rule us. Are we prepared for what that will cost? It will cost everything that is not of God in us.

—Oswald Chambers

# Taking Possession of Our Inheritance

> No man shall be able to stand before you all the days of your life; as I was with Moses, so I will be with you. I will not leave you nor forsake you.
>
> Only be strong and very courageous, that you may observe to do according to all the law which Moses My servant commanded you; do not turn from it to the right hand or to the left, that you may prosper wherever you go.
>
> —Joshua 1:5, 7

The wilderness journey of the Israelites and their entry into the Promised Land under the leadership of Joshua is an important theme in the Bible, and it applies to us today. At this point in Israel's history, the Israelites were out of Egypt but not yet in the Promised Land. This is a picture of our own pilgrimage toward our promised inheritance.

We are out of our Egypt, the bondage of sin, and are journeying through the wilderness toward our New Jerusalem, but have not yet arrived. We have been redeemed from sin but have not yet realized our full inheritance—the kingdom of God. We are in that time of salvation history known as "already and not yet." On one hand, our inheritance in Christ and the blessings of the kingdom of God are a present reality (Eph. 1:3). The Bible says:

> He has delivered us from the power of darkness and conveyed [transferred] us into the kingdom of the Son of His love, in whom we have redemption through His blood, the forgiveness of sins. Col. 1:13–14

On the other hand, the kingdom of God and our inheritance in Christ are a future blessing (1 Cor. 15:50; 1 Pet. 1:3–4). We will be ushered into the fullness of the kingdom of God for possessing our inheritance as joint heirs with Christ when Christ shall return in His glory. The apostle Peter wrote:

> Therefore, brethren, be even more diligent to make your call and election sure, for if you do these things you will never stumble; for so an entrance will be supplied to you abundantly into the everlasting kingdom of our Lord and Savior Jesus Christ. 2 Pet. 1:10–11

The apostle Paul echoed the same hope when he wrote, "In Him [Jesus] you also trusted, after you heard the word of truth, the gospel of your salvation; in whom also, having believed, you were sealed with the Holy Spirit of promise, who is the guarantee of our inheritance until the redemption of the purchased possession, to the praise of His glory" (Eph. 1:13–14).

God told Joshua to lead the Israelites into the land that He promised and already granted to His people. But they needed to go in and possess the land in faith. Though the commission given to Joshua looked daunting, the good news was that, with the divine commission, God also gave His promises. He gave three specific promises to the Israelites as they prepared to possess the Promised Land. These promises are just as relevant to us now as they were to the Israelites then as we press forward to possess our inheritance.

## THE PROMISE OF DIVINE PRESENCE

"No man shall be able to stand before you all the days of your life; as I was with Moses, so I will be with you. I will not leave you nor forsake you" (Josh. 1:5). The Lord assured Joshua of His presence. God said to Joshua that as He was with Moses, so He would be with him. What is in view here is not the omnipresence of God but the manifest presence of God—His presence in a tangible way to those who are in a covenant relationship with Him. We too need God's abiding presence if we are going to reach our destination and possess our inheritance.

God manifested His presence to Joshua by parting the Jordan River. Throughout the Old Testament, God manifested His presence in different ways—for example, the pillar of fire by night and the pillar of cloud in the wilderness; the parting of the Red Sea; providing Manna from heaven; and fire and thunder on Mount Sinai. But the supreme manifestation of God's presence with His people was the coming of the Lord Jesus Christ. Jesus is called Immanuel: "God with us." When He was on earth, He veiled His glory so that people could see the face of God and not die.

Jesus said: "He who has My commandments and keeps them, it is he who loves Me. And he who loves Me will be loved by My Father, and I will love him and manifest Myself to him" (John 14:21). The key to experiencing the manifest presence of God is to be obedient to His will. Jesus told His disciples of the coming of the Holy Spirit, the Comforter, who will dwell in them. Jesus is not with us in the flesh, but He is with us and in us by His Spirit. The indwelling presence of the Holy Spirit and His manifestation within and without is a New Covenant blessing.

The presence of God is manifested in different ways in the life of a believer. The Bible says that in the presence of the Lord is the fullness of joy (Ps. 16:11). You know that God's presence is with you when you have that abiding joy, even in the midst of the storms of life. Another manifestation of divine presence is unusual boldness. When the rulers, elders, and scribes, saw the boldness of uneducated and untrained Peter and John, they realized that they had been with Jesus. When the presence of Christ is with us, we experience unusual boldness. When the disciples prayed for boldness, the whole place where they were praying was shaken to display the presence of the Lord, and they were filled with the Holy Spirit and spoke with boldness (Acts 4:31).

God is with us when we do the assignment to which He has called us. Jesus said to His disciples, whom He commissioned to spread the gospel: "Lo I am with you always, even to the end of the age" (Matt. 28:20). If you are doing what God has assigned you, you can count on God's presence. What is your assignment at the present moment? Is it being a homemaker? Working in the office? Being a student? Being a preacher? You experience God's presence when you do it out of love for God and to display His excellence in all that you do. As Brother Lawrence, a cook in a French monastery, said, practice the presence of God daily wherever you are and whatever you do by offering all that you have for the glory of God. Brother Lawrence practiced the presence of God even in the mundane work of the kitchen.

## THE PROMISE OF DIVINE PRUDENCE

God said to Joshua, "Only be strong and very courageous, that you may observe to do according to all the law which Moses My servant commanded you; do not turn from it to the right hand or to the left, that you may prosper wherever you go" (Josh. 1:7). God repeated this promise three times to emphasize that Joshua needed to be strong and courageous.

The word "strong" literally means to be steadfast. The word "courageous" literally means to be resolute. God said to Joshua that he needed to be steadfast and resolute in his mission of entering into the Promised Land and not to be afraid of the enemies. And God said that to complete this mission, Joshua needed wisdom or prudence. The Greek word translated as "prosper" in Josh. 1:7 means to be prudent or wise. The Septuagint correctly translates the Hebrew word *sakal* to mean prudence.

C. S. Lewis calls "prudence" a cardinal virtue. It comes from the Latin word *cardinis*, which means "door hinge." Just as a door turns on its hinge and functions as it is supposed to, prudence is a pivotal virtue, because it enables us to evaluate what we are doing and what is likely to come of it. The apostle Paul understood the importance of prudence when he wrote, "See then that you walk circumspectly, not as fools but as wise" (Eph. 5:15–18). A prudent person understands what the will of God is and lives his or her life circumspectly and uses time wisely to accomplish the purposes of God.

How do we become prudent? Our text gives us the answer. God said to Joshua that if he did what Moses taught him to do and not turn to the left or to the right from the precepts of God, he would be wise and successful. To make a successful pilgrimage, we need wisdom, which comes when we meditate on the word of God. Joshua, the deliverer of Israel, needed to follow the law and become wise so he could lead his people. However, Jesus, the new "Joshua," who was the personification of wisdom, fulfilled the law without fail and is the source of all wisdom.

The Bible says in Him are hidden all the treasures of wisdom and knowledge (Col. 2:3). His wisdom is imparted to us by His Spirit who dwells in us. The apostle Paul calls the Holy Spirit the Spirit of wisdom and knowledge (Eph. 1:17). When the leaders of the Jerusalem church needed deacons to serve there, they said, "Seek among you seven men with good reputation and full of the Holy Spirit and wisdom" (Acts 6:3).

Are you living your life controlled and guided by the Holy Spirit? Do you seek His guidance when you reach the fork-of-the-road decision points in your life? It is impossible to travel this pilgrim's road without the aid of the Spirit of God and the Word of God. We need prudence to make progress in our pilgrim's journey and take possession of our inheritance.

## THE PROMISE OF DIVINE PROSPERITY

God said to Joshua: "This Book of the Law shall not depart from your mouth, but you shall meditate in it day and night, that you may observe to do according to all that is written in it. For then you will make your way prosperous, and then you will have good success" (Josh. 1:8). The Hebrew word *tsalach*, translated as "prosperous," in this text means to move forward to reach one's destiny. This word is used in Isaiah 55:11 to remind us that God's word will accomplish what it is intended to do by God. In the Septuagint, *tsalach* is translated by the Greek word *euodoo*, which Paul uses in the New Testament to refer to a successful journey.

> For God is my witness, whom I serve in my spirit in the gospel of His Son, that without ceasing I make mention of you always in my prayers, making request if, by some means, now at last I may find a way [*euodoo*] in the will of God to come to you. Rom. 1:9

In order to have a prosperous journey and reach our destination, we need to conduct ourselves in a way that is pleasing to God. In 1 Corinthians 10, the apostle Paul says that the children of Israel who left Egypt did not make it to the Promised Land but perished in the wilderness because God was not pleased with them: they lusted, committed sexual immorality, tempted God, complained, and committed idolatry. That's why Paul exhorts us to present our bodies a living sacrifice, holy and pleasing (*euarestos*) to God. The apostle John wrote that whatever we ask of God, we receive from Him because we keep His commandments and do what is pleasing in His sight (1 John. 3:22).

Is your life pleasing to God? Are your words meditations of your heart pleasing to God? What is your motivation for your Christian service? If your motive is not right and your heart is not in the right place, even your

Christian service is noxious to God. The truth is that no matter how hard you try, you cannot live a life that is pleasing to God unless God works in you both to will and to do for His good pleasure (Phil. 2:13).

We are delivered from our Egypt, but we have not arrived yet at our Promised Land. We are in our wilderness journey. We know that we will complete this journey because we have the promise of divine presence, divine prudence, and divine prosperity.

## PRAYER

*Dear Lord, I am a sojourner and pilgrim in this life. Help me to travel this pilgrim's pathway looking unto You and trusting in You. Keep me from the distractions and enticements of this world and help me to move forward in my journey with strength and perseverance. Amen.*

# Growing in Love

And behold, a certain lawyer stood up and tested Him,
saying, "Teacher, what shall I do to inherit eternal life?"
He said to him, "What is written in the law? What is your
reading of it?" So he answered and said, "You shall love
the Lord your God with all your heart, with all your soul,
with all your strength, and with all your mind,' and 'your
neighbor as yourself."

—Luke 10:25–27

On May 5, 2000, millions of people around the globe
unwittingly opened an email with the subject line
"ILOVEYOU" and an attachment entitled "LOVE-
LETTER-FOR-YOU." When the attachment was opened, it
activated a computer virus that corrupted their document,
image, and audio files. The virus also sent a copy of itself to
all the addresses in the user's address book. Computer experts
estimated that this virus caused $5–$10 billion in damage
worldwide. This all happened because those who opened this
email were fascinated to read that someone loved them, and
they wanted to know who it was.

We all want to love and be loved. Indeed, love is an intense expression of our being. This should not be surprising, for we are born with the capacity to love because God, who created us in His image, is love (1 John 4:8). Jesus said: "You shall love the Lord your God with all your heart, with all your soul, with all your strength, and with all your mind, and your neighbor as yourself" (Luke 10:27). Our ability to love others or seek their greater good, irrespective of who they are, flows out of our love for God. Loving God and loving others are inextricably cross-linked; we cannot do one without the other (1 John 4:20–21).

## STAGES OF LOVE

How do we grow in loving God and others? I found the insights of St. Bernard of Clairvaux (1090–1153), a French abbot who founded the Cistercian order, helpful in answering this question. In his treatise *On Loving God*, he wrote of the four stages or degrees of love.[1]

The first stage of love is to love oneself for self's sake. This is selfish love, where a person, like a newborn infant, only thinks of self-gratification. He or she is preoccupied with selfish interests. The way to keep in check this selfish love, according to St. Bernard, is by loving our neighbor, knowing that God is the source of love, and trusting Him for our personal needs.

The second stage of love is to love God for self's sake. Though we may think that we are self-made and can stand on our own, the reality is that sometimes we run into storms of life that move us to seek God's help. Our unmet needs drive us to God, and in the process, we experience His goodness. We soon learn that we cannot live independently of God and

---

1. Richard and James Smith Foster, ed., *Devotional Classics* (New York: HarperSanFrancisco, 1993), 40–45.

begin to love Him, even if that love is a means for meeting our needs.

In the third stage of love, we love God for God's sake. As we experience the goodness and grace of God, we learn who God is and love Him for Himself (Ps. 49:18). We no longer love God because of our necessity, but because we have tasted and seen how gracious the Lord is. Once we start loving God for Himself, it becomes easier to love our neighbor, for "whosoever loves God aright loves all God's creatures."[2]

The fourth stage of love is to love oneself for God's sake. At this stage, our will and affections are subsumed in God so that His will becomes ours. St. Bernard wrote, "How blessed is he who reaches the fourth degree of love, wherein one loves himself only in God!" As a drop of water poured into wine loses itself, we forget ourselves when we are transmuted into the will of God. We desire none but God, and whatever we do, we do for His sake (Ps. 73:25). It is at this point that we truly love God with all our heart, soul, mind, and strength.

## LOVING GOD AND OTHERS

Is it possible for us to love God and our neighbor perfectly in this life? Not really! Even in our redeemed state, we still live with a fallen nature and are subject to the cares and vicissitudes of life. We must await the return of Christ and our glorification for perfection. That being said, we must still seek to grow in loving God, others, and ourselves in obedience to the command of Christ. It is a journey that begins by embracing God's love that is lavished upon us on the cross. The Bible says, "We love Him because He first loved us" (1 John 4:19). He poured out His love in our hearts by the Holy Spirit who has been given to us (Rom. 5:5).

---

2. Christian History Institute, "#207: Bernard Clairvaux on Love," https://www.christianhistoryinstitute.org/study/module/bernard (accessed May 15, 2018).

The power to love others in a giving, forgiving, and unchanging way is a gift of the Holy Spirit (Rom. 5:5; Gal. 5:22). We make progress on this journey by living a relinquished life: that is, dying daily to self (1 Cor. 15:31), whereby we can say, "I have been crucified with Christ; it is no longer I who live, but Christ lives in me; and the life which I now live in the flesh I live by faith in the Son of God, who loved me and gave Himself for me." (Gal. 2:20).

## PRAYER

*Dear Lord, fill my heart with Your love that I may love You with all my heart, soul, strength, and mind. Help me grow in loving You in a way that Your will is all that I seek and want to do. And help me love others and myself for Your sake. In Christ's name, I pray. Amen.*

# Redeeming the Time

> See then that you walk circumspectly, not as fools but as
> wise, redeeming the time, because the days are evil.
> Therefore do not be unwise, but understand what the will
> of the Lord is.
>
> — Ephesians 5:15–16

Saint Augustine once quipped, "What then is time? If no
one asks me, I know what it is. If I wish to explain it to
him who asks, I do not know."[1]

If time eluded Augustine, it is even more elusive to us who
live in an Einsteinian universe, where we no longer have the
luxury to view time as an absolute construct. Yet, in our
mortality, we are mindful that our days are "swifter than a
weaver's shuttle" (Job 7:6). As Andrew Marvell, the
seventeenth-century British poet, eloquently noted, we sense
the irresistible rush of time: "But at my back I always hear

---

1. Attributed to St. Augustine. Quoted in Fred Allan Wolf, *Parallel
Universes: The Search for Other Worlds* (New York: Simon & Schuster
Paperbacks, 1988), 164.

Time's winged chariot hurrying near."[2] Oh, how we wish to stop the chariot of time so we can catch a little breath, but it keeps mercilessly and ruthlessly galloping forward with relentless speed!

Each of us bears the ravages of time in some measure on our body and soul. Whether we like it or not, we live with a nagging sense of what Alvin Toffler called the "death of permanence."[3] Henry Gariepy, in his essay "The Brevity of Time," notes: "Time indeed steals our years and life away. It will write wrinkles on our faces, scribble crow's feet about our eyes, and paint our hair white. It is the one preacher to whom all must listen. Professor Time, that venerable pedagogue, teaches his lessons well."[4] Because our lives are inextricably linked to how we mark the passing of time, it is a matter of utmost urgency that we know how to respond to Professor Time.

The Bible says, "See then that you walk circumspectly, not as fools but as wise, redeeming the time, because the days are evil" (Eph. 5:15). Paul exhorts us to redeem our time because we are living in an evil age that is morally and spiritually bankrupt (Gal. 1:4). Indeed, we are seeing an intense proliferation of evil all around us—debauchery, wars, famine, natural disasters, and the breaking of the family. The list goes on. We don't have to look far to find evil.

## WALK CAREFULLY

The verb *exagorazo* (redeem) in Eph. 5:16 literally means "buy in the market" or "buy out of the market." This expression was used in biblical days to describe the buying and freeing of a slave from the slave market. The basic idea, as it applies to

---

2. A line from Andrew Marvell's poem *To His Coy Mistress*.

3. Alvin Toffler, *Future Shock* (New York: Bantam Books, Inc., 1970), 7.

4. Henry Gariepy, *Portraits of Perseverance* (Wheaton: Victor Books, 1989), 66.

time, is that we must liberate or rescue our time from the bondage of mindless, purposeless, unproductive, and God-dishonoring activities. The time of our life is the most important asset God has given us; therefore, we must constantly evaluate how we are spending our time and seek to make the most positive use of it.

In our fallen state, however, we lack the moral ability or what the Bible calls liberty to free our time from its bondage. Though we have the natural ability to make choices, in our state of spiritual deadness we freely make sinful choices. We find sin more desirable than the things of God. What needs to happen, then, is for us to be "made alive" or liberated (*libertas*) in Christ before we can redeem our time and invest it for God's purposes. Paul exhorts: "Stand fast therefore in the liberty by which Christ has made us free, and do not be entangled again with a yoke of bondage" (Gal. 5:1).

Like the Israelites of old, we must be freed from Egypt before we can receive the law of God for living. That's why Jesus came to seek and to save the lost. Have you received the saving grace of Christ? Remember, God graciously saves us in Christ before He graciously calls us to live for Christ.

## PRAYER

*Lord, teach me to use my time wisely to bring honor and glory to Your name. Give me victory over distractions that keep me from doing things that please You. In Christ's name, I pray. Amen.*

# Reverential Obedience

Will you not receive instruction to obey My words? Says the Lord. The words of Jonadab the son of Rechab, which he commanded hos sons, not to drink wine are performed; for this day they drink none, and obey their father's commandment. But although I have spoken to you, rising early and speaking, you did not obey Me.

— Jeremiah 35:14

Leonard Ravenhill, the famous English preacher, said, "Spiritual maturity comes not by erudition, but by compliance with the known will of God."[1] Explicit obedience to the commandments of God is the heartbeat of the Christian life.

The prophet Samuel admonished the Israelites: "What is more pleasing to the Lord: your burnt offerings and sacrifices or your obedience to his voice? Listen! Obedience is better

---

1. Sherwood Wirt and Kersten Beckstrom, *Topical Encyclopedia of Living Quotations* (Minneapolis: Bethany House Publishers, 1982), 165.

than sacrifice, and submission is better than offering the fat of rams. Rebellion is as sinful as witchcraft, and stubbornness as bad as worshipping idols" (1 Sam. 15:22–23 NLT). Jesus said, "If you love me, obey my commandments...When you obey my commandments, you remain in my love, just as I obey my Father's commandments and remain in his love" (John 14:15; 15:10 NLT).

If obedience is so vital to our Christian life, how are we to engage in this all-important spiritual discipline? The story of the Recabites recorded in Jeremiah 35 gives us an excellent biblical framework for practicing the spiritual discipline of obedience. God was grieved by the disobedience and apostasy of the kingdom of Judah and wanted to teach Israel a lesson on obedience. God told Jeremiah to summon the Recabites to the Temple of God and offer them wine to drink.

Who were these Rechabites? They were a nomadic people who descended from Jonadab, son of Rechab. More than two hundred years earlier, Jonadab had commanded his sons not to drink wine, build houses, or plant vineyards, but always to live in tents. That is exactly what the Recabites had been doing when they were brought to the Lord's Temple. When Jeremiah set the cups and jugs of wine before them and asked them to drink, they refused, saying that they would not disobey the command of their forefather. The kingdom of Judah could not have received a more powerful object lesson on obedience than that. God said: "The Recabites do not drink wine to this day because their ancestor Jehonadab told them not to. But I have spoken to you again and again, and you refuse to obey me" (Jer. 35:14 NLT).

The obedience of the Recabites to the command of Jonadab points to an important but often overlooked aspect of biblical obedience. When the Rechabites were asked to drink wine, they said that they would not drink because their ancestor Jonadab had commanded them not to drink wine (Jer. 35:6). Their reverence and respect for Jonadab was the reason for obeying his command.

In contrast, the kingdom of Judah continued to disobey God in spite of His repeated warnings about their irreverence towards Him. God lamented over Judah saying, "Even an ox knows its owner, and a donkey recognizes its master's care—but Israel doesn't know its master. My people don't recognize my care for them" (Is. 1:3 NLT). God was grieved by their irreverence. Reverence for God is the catalyst for obedience.

## OBEDIENCE IS HOLY REVERENCE

Reverence is an attitude of the heart and is the basis of all moral values. It enables us to grasp moral virtues and subordinate our egotistical self to God. As Dietrich and Alice von Hildebrand put it so eloquently, "without a fundamental attitude of reverence, no true love, no justice, no kindness, no self-development, no purity, no truthfulness, are possible; above all, without reverence, the dimension of depth is completely excluded…It is the basis for the right attitude of men toward themselves, their neighbors, to every level of being, and above all to God"[2]

We learn that obedience to God flows out of reverence for God—a "holy fear." When Potiphar's wife seductively pressured Joseph to sleep with her, he refused, saying, "How could I do such a wicked thing? It would be a great sin against God" (Gen. 39:9 NLT). Potiphar's wife may have planned for all contingencies, but as far as Joseph was concerned, even if no one knew what happened behind closed doors, God would know it. And his reverence for God kept him from yielding to the temptation.

The Bible teaches that the fear of the Lord (reverence) is the beginning of wisdom, and the wisest thing a person can do is to obey the Lord. So if we are to live a life of obedience to God, the first step is to inculcate a holy fear of, or reverence for, God—something which is profoundly lacking

2. Dietrich von Hildebrand and Alice von Hildebrand, *The Art of Living* (Chicago: Henry Regnery Company, 1965), 9.

in modern Christendom. But we are fundamentally irreverent creatures. Our irreverence is rooted in our pride and our insatiable desire for self-gratification. The apostle Paul wrote: "No one is righteous—not even one. No one is truly wise; no one is seeking God. All have turned away; all have become useless. No one does good, not a single one" (Rom. 3:11–18 NLT). This spirit of disobedience entered the human experience when our first parents disobeyed the express command of God in the Garden of Eden. As a result, mankind is "locked up in disobedience" (Rom. 11:32). The Bible teaches that "For as in Adam all die, even so in Christ all shall be made alive" (1 Cor. 15:22).

While the first Adam plunged us into disobedience from which we could not rescue ourselves, the last Adam, Jesus Christ, came to rescue us from a life of disobedience. By His perfect obedience to the Father's will, His atoning death on the cross, and His resurrection, Christ proved that He alone is able to free us from the bondage of disobedience. Therefore, to have the Spirit of Christ means to have the power to obey the commandments of God.

Obedience to God's revealed will is the flip side of faith. The Bible says that without faith it is impossible to please God (Heb. 11:6). A life that is pleasing to God is a life of obedience. Faith and obedience are inseparable. Dietrich Bonhoeffer, the German theologian, insightfully observed: "Only those who obey can believe, and only those who believe can obey."[3] Obedience is also the precondition for growing in the knowledge of God. The more we obey what is already revealed to us in His word, the better we grasp the deeper things of God and grow in the knowledge of God. True listening to God's word occurs when hearing becomes obedience.

---

3. Dietrich Bonhoeffer, *The Cost of Discipleship* (New York: Simon & Schuster, 1959), 70.

If God has been speaking to you on any particular matter through His word and you have been ignoring it, you are walking in disobedience. Repent of your disobedience without delay and turn to God with reverence. The psalmist prayed, "I thought about my ways, and turned my feet to your testimonies. I made haste, and did not delay to keep Your commandments" (Ps. 119:60). Let this be our constant prayer.

## PRAYER

*Lord, teach me to be obedient to Your word and do that which is pleasing in Your sight. Help me to be filled with the knowledge of Your will. Amen.*

# The Barzillai Challenge

> Now it happened, when David had come to Mahanaim,
> that Shobi the son of Nahash from Rabbah of the people
> of Ammon, Machir the son of Ammiel from Lo-debar,
> and Barzillai the Gileadite from Rogelim, brought beds
> and basins, earthen vessels and wheat, barley and flour,
> parched grain and beans, lentils and parched seeds, honey
> and curds, sheep and cheese of the herd, for David and the
> people who were with him to eat. For they said, "The
> people are hungry and weary and thirsty in the wilderness."
>
> —2 Samuel 17:27–29

Have you heard of Barzillai? No, I don't mean Godzilla, but Barzillai. You may not have heard of Barzillai, but there really was a man with that name, which means "my iron." You can read about him in 2 Samuel 17 and 19. He was an Israelite from Gilead. David's son Absalom and a band of 200 men had been planning to dethrone David and take over the kingdom of Israel. According to their plan, they went to Hebron with the pretense to offer sacrifices to the Lord. While they were there, Absalom sent secret messengers to all the tribes of Israel to stir up revolt against David. "As soon as you hear the ram's horn," his message read, "you are to say, 'Absalom has been crowned king in Hebron.'" Thus Absalom declared himself king of Israel and started pursuing David.

When David was told that all of Israel had joined with Absalom to conspire against him, David and his household, bodyguards, and 600 men from Gath fled Jerusalem. He left no one behind except ten of his concubines to look after the palace. He told the men from Gath to join Absalom because they were foreigners in exile in Israel. Moreover, said David, he was not sure where he was going to go after leaving Jerusalem or what the future held. But the men from Gath refused to leave him. Instead, they renewed their pledge to support David and vowed to go with him wherever the Lord led him, no matter what happened. So David and his men crossed the Kidron Valley, walked up the road to the Mount of Olives, and crossed the Jordan River to reach Mahanaim in the region of Gilead.

At this point, Absalom had mobilized the entire army of Israel and was leading his troops across the Jordan River. After crossing, they reached the land of Gilead near Mahanaim where David was hiding. When David and his men reached Mahanaim, they were exhausted. They were out of food and water. Some of the men may have been ill as a result of wandering through the hot desert. To their pleasant surprise, Barzillai, a rich 80-year-old man with impaired hearing, entered and warmly welcomed David, providing him and his hundreds of men with sheep and goats, various food items, water, cooking pots, serving bowls, and sleeping mats. He said, "You must all be very hungry, tired, and thirsty after your long march through the wilderness." Needless to say, David was very grateful for the timely help that he received from Barzillai.

Barzillai may have had many noteworthy accomplishments to his credit. But God chose to immortalize his name for an act of kindness that he showed at the ripe old age of eighty. He provided David and his men with food and water in their hour of need. By this exemplary service, Barzillai presents us with a challenge to serve in a way that is pleasing to our King, the Lord Jesus.

## SERVE RESPONSIVELY

First, we must serve responsively. Barzillai saw a need and responded to meet that need according to his ability and the resources God had given him. He could have ignored the need and not get involved because of his old age, physical limitations, and the possibility of invoking the anger of Absalom for helping David. He was not deterred by any of these limitations or potential risks. He saw a need and met it according to his ability despite his old age when most people would have preferred to live a life of quiet, peace, and rest. If Barzillai had not reached out to help in that critical period in David's life, David might well have perished in the desert and the history of Israel would have been different.

Barzillai challenges us to look around for those who are in need! When we do, we will see people with all kinds of needs—homeless people, hungry people, tired people, people in need of encouragement, people with illnesses, people in nursing homes, young people who need mentoring, newly converted Christians who need to be discipled, a foreign student who is feeling homesick, shut-ins who need a meal, and people who need to hear the gospel. The list is limitless. We must perceive the need around us and do what we can to meet that need.

We serve King Jesus who descended from David and inherited an eternal throne (Is. 9:7; Luke 1:32). Jesus said that when we help those who are in need, even if it is offering a cup of cold water, we are doing it unto the Lord (Matt. 25:40; 10:42). The Barzillai challenge calls us to help those in need according to our ability and the grace God gives us.

## SERVE GENEROUSLY

Second, we must serve generously. Without regard for his own personal needs, Barzillai liberally provided David and his men food, water, and other supplies they needed. Granted, he was a rich man and could afford to give what David needed. But being wealthy does not automatically predispose one to generosity. Earlier, David had asked Nabal, a wealthy man, to help him and his men for protecting Nabal's shepherds from the attack of nearby marauding bands while they were tending their flock in Carmel. David's servants requested, "Please give whatever comes to your hand to your servants and to your son David."

But Nabal refused to help, saying, "Who is David, and who is the son of Jesse? There are many servants nowadays who break away each one from his master. Shall I then take my bread and my water and my meat that I have killed for my shearers, and give it to men when I do not know where they are from?" (1 Sam. 25:10–11). Nabal was rich, but he did not have the spirit of liberality.

The church at Macedonia eagerly and generously sent monetary help to the church at Jerusalem when they were going through a famine. They offered their assistance, not because they were rich, but because they first gave themselves to the Lord. Moreover, they gave "according to their ability, yes, and beyond their ability, they were freely willing" (2 Cor. 8:3). Helping others in their hour of need is a gift of grace. It takes the grace of God to keep us from looking the other way when confronted with a need. The Bible says, "Do not withhold good from those to whom it is due, when it is in the power of your hand to do so" (Prov. 3:27).

## SERVE SELFLESSLY

Third, we must serve selflessly. Barzillai had no hidden agenda in helping David. He expected no favors from David for providing food and water. But David did not forget the generosity of Barzillai. When David heard that Absalom had died, he mourned for his son with great pathos and wished that he had died in his place. After grieving for his son, David decided to return to Jerusalem. Barzillai came down from Rogelim to escort David across the Jordan. "Come across with me and live in Jerusalem," the king said to Barzillai. "I will take care of you there." "No," he replied, "I am far too old to go with the king to Jerusalem." Barzillai told David that he was too old to make the journey to Jerusalem and was no longer able to enjoy the good things of life. He said that just to go across the Jordan River with the king was all the honor he needed. Barzillai asked the king to take his servant, Chimham, with him to receive whatever good things the king wanted to give him. He did not seek to grab the honor that was his to take. Instead, he selflessly relinquished the honor of going with the king so that his servant Chimham could receive it.

Barzillai exemplifies for us in a small measure that when we serve others responsively, generously, and selflessly, God is always well pleased. The paragon of such service in all of human history was Jesus Christ. He saw our helpless, lost state and responded to our need by coming down to rescue us. The Bible says, "For the Son of Man has come to seek and to save that which was lost" (Luke 19:10). Jesus sacrificed Himself for our sins that we may receive His generous gift of salvation. He selflessly gave Himself for our redemption.

The Bible says, "Though he was God, he did not think of equality with God as something to cling to. Instead, he gave up his divine privileges; he took the humble position of a slave and was born as a human being. When he appeared in human form, he humbled himself in obedience to God and died a criminal's death on a cross" (Phil. 2:6–8 NLT).

We can meet the Barzillai challenge authentically only when we are moved by the grace of the Lord Jesus Christ. He alone is able to empower us and ennoble us to serve others responsively, generously, and selflessly.

## PRAYER

*Lord, give me a servant's heart and help me to see the world around me through Your eyes. Grant me the courage to respond to the needs I see according to the grace and ability You give me. Help me to serve my fellow man selflessly and generously with what I have for Your glory. Amen.*

# The Power of Silence

He who has knowledge spares his words,
And a man of understanding is of a calm spirit.
Even a fool is counted wise when he holds his peace;
When he shuts his lips, he is considered perceptive.

—Proverbs 17:27–28

In the text before us, Solomon extols the virtue of silence. He is not advocating absolute silence, but rather the discipline of using our words sparingly. Perhaps a better description of this virtue is "judicious silence." What is most noteworthy is that a case for judicious silence is being made by a man who was known for his Niagara of words that touches every aspect of our life.

We are, indeed, creatures of words. In fact, we are the sum total of words spoken by us and spoken to us. It is impossible to conceive a world of humanity without words. We use words to express our feelings of joy and sorrow; to tell a truth or a lie; to comfort one another; to make promises and spread gossip. We use words to cover our inadequacies and trumpet our accomplishments. We say words to break up the silence when we are with a stranger. It is estimated that on the average we speak approximately 370 million words in our lifetime.

The world, as we know it, began with words. The Bible teaches that God brought form, order, and life to the earth by His spoken word (Genesis 1). He made the ages (eons) by speaking His word (*rhema*), and by faith, we understand that the things that are seen were not made of things that do appear (Heb. 11:3). At the time of creation, the morning stars sang together and the angels shouted for joy (Job 38:7). The mighty seraphim flew day and night around the throne of God in worship saying, "Holy, holy, holy is the Lord of Heaven's Armies! The whole earth is filled with his glory!" (Is. 6:3 NLT). Thus all of heaven and earth resonate with words, words, and words!

Despite the indispensability and power of words, we find ourselves in life situations when words are simply inadequate to express our thoughts and feelings. In such situations, we speak volumes with our silence. The American novelist Herman Melville wrote, "All profound things and emotions of things are preceded and attended by Silence."[1] Martin Farquhar Tupper (1810–1889), the English poet and writer of proverbial philosophy, said, "Well-timed silence hath more eloquence than speech."[2]

In Psalm 19:1–4, we read that the heavens declare the glory of God. They speak in silence, and though their voice is not heard, their message goes throughout the earth. When we are in awe, we are speechless. Similarly, the Bible admonishes us, "But the Lord is in His holy temple. Let all the earth keep silence before Him" (Hab. 2:20). Solomon advises:

---

1. Wisdom Commons, http://www.wisdomcommons.org/ wisbits/5249-all-profound-things-and-emotions (accessed December 2, 2016).

2. The Quotations Page, http://www.quotationspage.com/ subjects/silence (accessed December 2, 2016).

Do not be rash with your mouth,
And let not your heart utter anything
hastily before God.
For God is in heaven, and you on earth;
Therefore let your words be few. Eccl. 5:2

The power of silence is often neglected in our culture of noise, crowds, and hurry. In our text, Solomon brings to our attention three noteworthy virtues of judicious silence.

## SILENCE REVEALS WISDOM

First, judicious silence reveals our wisdom. We read: "He who has knowledge spares his words." The Hebrew word *daath*, commonly translated as "knowledge," more accurately means insight, prudence, understanding, or wisdom. While knowledge helps us with what to say, wisdom enables us to know when to say it. This means that a wise person keeps silent until the appropriate time. The Bible says, "In the multitude of words sin is not lacking, but he who restrains his lips is wise" (Prov. 10:19). The apostle James exhorts: "So then, my beloved brethren, let every man be swift to hear, slow to speak, slow to wrath; for the wrath of man does not produce the righteousness of God" (James 1:19).

When the Second Continental Congress assembled in 1775 in Philadelphia, Pennsylvania, to debate whether or not the American colonies should declare independence from Britain, one of the participants of that Congress was Benjamin Franklin. While the delegates debated the matter intensely, Benjamin Franklin sat there in silence most of the time and did not participate in the arguments. Some of the delegates wondered if he was for independence or loyal to the British Crown.

Finally, after a long period of silence, when Franklin got up and said that he supported independence from Britain, his position was given extra attention and serious consideration, especially by delegates who were leaning toward Britain, because they assumed that Benjamin Franklin arrived at his decision not hastily but after careful thought. His prolonged silence and deliberate statement at the appropriate time was received as a mark of great wisdom. In the end, the Congress agreed to declare independence from the British Crown and the revolutionary war with Great Britain started.[3] Mahatma Gandhi (1869–1948) said it well: "In the attitude of silence the soul finds the path in a clear light, and what is elusive and deceptive resolves itself into crystal clearness. Our life is a long and arduous quest after Truth."[4]

When Job's three friends heard of the calamity of Job, they came to mourn with him and comfort him. They sat with him for seven days and seven nights and said nothing. No volume of words could have comforted Job. The wisest thing they did was to remain silent. But the moment they opened their mouth, they began to disclose their ignorance, foolishness, and misunderstanding of God's sovereignty and providence.

At one point, Job was so disgusted with their diagnosis of the cause of his calamities, he rebuked them, saying, "But you forgers of lies, you are all worthless physicians. Oh, that you would be silent and it would be your wisdom" (Job 13:4–5). Jobs friends were wiser in their silence than in their speech. An old Arab proverb says, "The wise are dumb; silence is wisdom."

## SILENCE DISPLAYS SELF-CONTROL

Second, judicious silence displays our self-control. Solomon said, "And a man of understanding is of a calm spirit." The Hebrew word *qar*, translated as "calm," means cool, serene, or self-possessed. The New Living Translation Bible reads as

---

3. Kenneth Lange, "Silence: How to Act Like a Wise Man," *Ben Franklin*, http://www.kennethlange.com/benjamin_franklin/html (accessed January 30, 2014; site now discontinued).

4. The Quotations Page, http://www.quotationspage.com/ subjects/silence (accessed December 3, 2016).

follows: "A truly wise person uses few words; a person of understanding is even-tempered." If wisdom is revealed by judicious silence, it stands to reason that a man of understanding would exercise judicious silence as a display of self-control.

The talented Publilius Syrus, a first-century BC Assyrian slave in Italy, was known for his wit and insightful proverbs. He won the favor of his master, who freed and educated him. Publilius Syrus said, "Speech is a mirror of the soul; as a man speaks, so is he."[5] He also said, "I have often regretted my speech, never my silence."[6] When we are angry or offended at someone, our first reaction is to respond in kind with words. And in the heat of the moment, we say words that we regret later, but we cannot take back the words we have said. The apostle James wrote, "For we all stumble in many things. If anyone does not stumble in word, he is a perfect man, able also to bridle the whole body" (James 3:2).

Silence is an effective method of self-control. Making silence our first response gives us an opportunity to reflect and gather our thoughts together and keeps us from reacting irrationally or emotionally toward an offender. The Bible says, "Whoever guards his mouth and tongue keeps his soul from troubles" (Prov. 21:23).

When Jesus was brought before the high priest Caiaphas, a false witness came forward and said that he heard Jesus saying, "I am able to destroy the temple of God and to build it in three days." When the high priest asked Him to respond to this charge, Jesus kept silent. What Jesus actually said was, "Destroy this temple, and in three days I will raise it up" (John 2:19). Jesus was speaking of His body, not the temple in Jerusalem. He exercised self-control by keeping silent

---

5. The Quotations Page, http://www.quotationspage.com /quotes/Publilius_Syrus/31 (accessed December 3, 2016).

6. The Quotations Page, http://www.quotationspage.com /quotes/Publilius_Syrus/11 (accessed December 3, 2016).

instead of lashing at His accusers. The apostle Peter exhorts us to follow the example of Christ, "who, when He was reviled, did not revile in return; when He suffered, He did not threaten, but committed Himself to Him who judges righteously" (1 Pet. 2:23).

## SILENCE CONCEALS FOOLISHNESS

Third, judicious silence conceals our foolishness. Our text says, "Even a fool is counted wise when he holds his peace; when he shuts his lips, he is considered perceptive" (Prov. 17:28). When silence is judiciously exercised, it reveals wisdom. Conversely, it also conceals one's foolishness. Once, David sent his young men to Nabal, a wealthy man who had lots of sheep and goats. It was sheep-shearing time, so the men went to Nabal to ask if he would be kind enough to share some of his provisions with David as a reward for protecting his sheep and shepherds when they were near Carmel.

Nabal should have considered David's request. The least he could have done was to keep silent and conceal his arrogance and foolishness. Instead, he chose to live up to the meaning of his name (fool). He berated the young men and called David an outlaw and a freeloader. That was the undoing of Nabal, who let his ill-temper go wild. Mark Twain said, "It is better to remain silent and be thought a fool than to open one's mouth and remove all doubt."[7]

The power of silence must be learned and diligently practiced. The best place to learn it is in the presence of God. "A man who loves God, necessarily loves silence," wrote Thomas Merton.[8] The prophet Zechariah announced, "Be silent, all flesh, before the Lord, for He is aroused from His

---

7. Brainy Quote, http://www.brainyquote.com/quotes/quotes/m/marktwain103535.html (accessed December 3, 2016).

8. Thomas McDonnell (ed), *A Thomas Merton Reader* (Doubleday: New York, 1974), 460.

holy habitation!" (Zech. 2:13). Let us be still in His presence and seek to know Him. Let us trust God to give us the grace to exercise judicious silence for His glory and honor.

## PRAYER

*Dear Lord, teach me to be quick to hear and slow to speak. Empower me to restrain my mouth, lest I sin with my tongue. And when I do speak, let my speech always be with grace as though it is seasoned with salt. In Christ's name, I pray. Amen.*

# The Released Life

And Moses said to the people, "Do not be afraid. Stand still, and see the salvation of the Lord, which He will accomplish for you today. For the Egyptians whom you see today, you shall see again no more forever. The Lord will fight for you, and you shall hold your peace."

— Exodus 14:13–14

D o you feel you are in a pressure-cooker these days? Your stream of finances is slowly drying up, and your job is not getting any easier. You are inundated with deadlines that you can't meet, and your boss is getting increasingly impatient with you. Or perhaps you are in search of employment and you can't seem to find a breakthrough. You feel trapped, pushed against the wall, with no sign of relief. Perhaps you are at a low point in your life due to an intractable illness and you don't know where to turn. I don't know what specific challenges or difficulties you may be facing at this moment in your life, but I want to assure you that help is on the way. If you feel imprisoned in your circumstances, you are not alone.

Long ago, Moses and the Israelites found themselves in a crisis with no exit sign. After nearly 430 years of bondage and slavery in Egypt, they found freedom because of God's powerful intervention. They were on their way to the Promised Land with a merry heart. But before long, they found themselves trapped between the Red Sea and the encroaching army of Pharaoh behind them. All around them was the barren desert. But God did not forget the Israelites, nor was His grace and power insufficient to sustain them. God told Moses to instruct the people to do three things. What they did then, you must do now to experience the release you are looking for.

## FACING LIFE'S CHALLENGES

First, you must face your difficulties with a holy boldness. Moses said to the people, "Do not be afraid." Moses encouraged the people to have faith in God, who redeemed them by His mighty power. Holy boldness comes not out of self-confidence, but from knowing who you are in Christ and to whom you belong. The Bible says, "You are of God, little children, and have overcome them, because He who is in you is greater than he who is in the world" (1 John 4:4). Face your challenges with a holy boldness, not with fear and timidity, because you belong to God almighty.

Second, you must face your difficulties with a holy stillness. Moses said to the people, "Stand still." In Hebrew, this expression literally means to stand your ground as firmly as a wall. Stand for truth and your principles. In times of difficulty, there is always the temptation to compromise your values and the truth deposited in you. Therefore, stand your ground. Why? Your salvation is of the Lord. Stand firmly and watch God make every mountain and hill in your life low, the crooked places plain, the rough places smooth, as He reveals His glory to you (Is. 40:4–5). Holy stillness is an expression of your trust in God's faithfulness.

Third, you must face your difficulties with a holy calmness. Moses said to the people, "The Lord will fight for you, and you shall hold your peace" (Ex. 14:14). The Hebrew root word for "peace" in this text has the idea of being silent while a plan is being devised. Hold your peace and remain calm while God is working behind the scenes to extract you from your predicament. Holy calmness lets you remain without anxiety, knowing that the battle is the Lord's (Phil. 4:6–7). He is at work on your behalf.

Friend, go forward now as a released individual. God has given you in Christ a holy boldness, a holy stillness, and a holy calmness to face your daily challenges.

## PRAYER

*Lord, enable me to face life with a holy boldness, a holy stillness, and holy calmness. In Jesus' name, I pray. Amen.*

# Walking Your Way to Health

> As you therefore have received Christ Jesus the Lord, so walk in Him, rooted and built up in Him and established in the faith, as you have been taught, abounding in it with thanksgiving.
>
> — Colossians 2:6–7

A few years ago, my wife and I went to visit a family member in a sleepy Midwestern town. Because the place where we were staying was surrounded by farms, I took my morning exercise walks in the nearby soya fields. It was quite exhilarating to walk in the fields, hear the birds chirp in the air, and feel the morning breeze softly caress my face.

During one such walk, I thought of Isaac of old: "And Isaac went out to meditate in the field in the evening" (Gen. 24:63). Oh! I could understand why Isaac chose to walk in the field, for the simple beauty of a verdant earth and the glory of a colorful meadow can surely invoke God's sweet presence and fire our spirit to commune with Him. George Washington Carver said it well: "Reading about nature is fine, but if a person walks in the woods and listens carefully, he can learn more than what is in the books, for they speak with the voice of God."[1]

The Bible speaks of a different kind of walk that is of eternal significance and is indispensable to our spiritual health. The apostle Paul wrote, "As you therefore have received Christ Jesus the Lord, so walk in Him, rooted and built up in Him and established in the faith, as you have been taught, abounding in it with thanksgiving" (Col. 2:6–7).

In this verse, Paul used an agricultural and an architectural metaphor to describe the essence of the Christian life—a life that is nourished by Christ and built on Christ. Jesus used the analogy of a vine and its branches to say that apart from Him we have no life (John 15:5). "Christ is our inseparable life," said Ignatius of Antioch, the first-century church father, "our life forever, our true life."[2] So, then, walking in Christ means to live in a vital union with Christ (John 14:20; Gal. 2:20).

## OUR UNION WITH CHRIST

How is our union with Christ translated into everyday living? First, it is demonstrated in our walk before God in truth. God said to Abraham, "I am Almighty God; walk before Me and be blameless" (Gen. 17:1). The Hebrew word *tawmeem*, translated as "blameless," literally means to walk with integrity. To walk before God means to live with the realization that we are under divine inspection (2 Chr. 16:9) and that God desires truth in our inner being (Ps. 51:6). Without truth, we cannot stand before a holy God or offer an acceptable worship to Him (Ps. 24:3–4; Jn. 4:23). Remember, your life is an open book before Him.

To be sure, union with Christ is more than walking before

---

1. Brainy Quote, https://www.brainyquote.com/quotes/quotes/g/georgewash140722.html (accessed December 3, 2016).

2. Quoted in Thomas Oden, *Life in the Spirit: Systematic Theology*, vol. 3 (Harper Collins, 1994), 205.

God; it also involves walking with God. "Enoch walked with God three hundred years" (Gen. 5:22). "Noah was a just man, perfect in his generations. Noah walked with God" (Gen. 6:9). Walking with God signifies our fellowship with Him. Our union with Christ is the basis of our communion with Him. Can two walk together without an agreement? (Amos 3:3).

Our union with Christ also enables us to walk after God in obedience to His will. "You shall walk after the Lord your God and fear Him, and keep His commandments" (Deut. 13:4). The apostle John trumpets the same exhortation in 1 John 3:22. When we walk after God, we submit to the Lordship of Christ and obey God's revealed will. The Bible says, "As you therefore have received Christ Jesus the Lord, so walk in Him" (Col. 2:6).

Have you received Christ as the Lord of your life? If not, will you take that first step towards walking in Christ? Now is the time. Tomorrow may be too late!

## PRAYER

*Lord, help me walk in fellowship with You daily. Help me walk in the integrity of my heart before You and in obedience to Your will after You. Let nothing come in the way of my walk with You. In Christ's name, I pray. Amen.*

# We Are Called to be Holy

I am the Lord your God. You shall therefore consecrate yourselves, and you shall be holy; for I am holy….For I am the Lord who brings you up out of the land of Egypt, to be your God. You shall therefore be holy, for I am holy.

—Leviticus 11:44–45

…But as He who called you is holy, you also be holy in all your conduct, because it is written, "Be holy, for I am holy."…Knowing that you were not redeemed with corruptible things, like silver or gold, from your aimless conduct received by tradition from your fathers, but with the precious blood of Christ, as of a lamb without blemish and without spot.

—1 Peter 1:15–16, 18

"Be holy, for I am holy" is a divine injunction given to all who are redeemed by the blood of Jesus Christ. Yet many Christians are not sure what biblical holiness means or how it applies to their lives. Some think that to be holy means to be cloistered in a monastery or live by a set of restrictive rules.

115

Recently, George Barna and associates conducted a survey of Christians that asked the respondents what it means to be holy. One out of five participants simply said: "I don't know." Others gave a wide range of responses, such as holiness is: being Christ-like, living a sinless life, making God your priority, having a good attitude toward people, being born again, or being guided by the Holy Spirit. Seven percent of the respondents said it means to reflect the character of God. Interestingly, the responses of born-again and non-born-again adults were identical in this survey. Barna concludes that many Christians attend church and read the Bible, but do not "understand the concept or significance of holiness, do not personally desire to be holy, and therefore do little, if anything, to pursue it."[1]

## THE MANDATE TO BE HOLY

From our text, we learn three truths about holiness. First, we learn of the mandate to be holy. God says, "I am the Lord your God. You shall therefore consecrate yourselves, and you shall be holy; for I am holy" (Lev. 11:44). This is an imperative, a command, and a requirement of God. After God delivered the Israelites from their bondage in Egypt, He told them that if they would obey Him and keep His covenant, then they would be to Him a kingdom of priests and a holy nation (Ex. 19:6). The apostle Paul wrote, "He chose us in Him [Christ] before the foundation of the world that we should be holy and without blame before Him in love" (Eph. 1:4). The Bible says, "Pursue peace with all people, and holiness, without which no one will see the Lord" (Heb. 12:14). It is God's will that we are holy (1 Thess. 4:3).

What does it mean to be holy? The Hebrew word *quadash*, translated as "holy" in Lev. 11:44 and elsewhere in the Bible,

---

1. Barna Group, "The Concept of Holiness Baffles Most Americans," https://www.barna.com/research/the-concept-of-holiness-baffles-most-americans (accessed December 3, 2016).

primarily conveys the idea of separation or of being set apart for a specific purpose. This Hebrew word is derived from the root *qad*, which means to "cut" or "separate." It is one of the most important words in the Old Testament. The Greek word *hagios*, translated as "holy" in 1 Pet. 1:16, also has the same meaning of separation and consecration.

Here is a practical example of being "set apart for a specific purpose." In Washington D.C., two great buildings—the Ritz Carlton Hotel and the White House—are both quite impressive in terms of their accommodations and appointments. But there is a difference. Anyone with money can book a room at the Ritz Carlton and stay there. But the White House is set apart for the President and his family.

God is holy because He is completely Other than what He has created. The Sabbath is holy because it is different from the rest of the days of the week and is set apart for a specific purpose (Ex. 20:8). In the Old Testament Tabernacle, certain objects and furnishings were deemed holy because they were set apart for specific tasks associated with worship. The ethical and moral dimension of holiness is also firmly connected to the notion of separation. The Bible says that no one is holy like the Lord, and there is no rock like our God (1 Sam. 2:2). God is wholly separated from all that is evil and sinful (Job. 34:10; Hab. 1:13). The Bible teaches that God is light and in Him is no darkness at all (1 John 1:5).

When God commands us to be holy, He means we should be separated from the sinfulness of this world and be consecrated unto Him. We are not to have fellowship with the unfruitful works of darkness, but be separated unto God (2 Cor. 6:17; Eph. 5:11). The Lord who called Israel to be holy also summons us, the new Israel in Christ, to be holy in all our conduct, whether in business or leisure, labor or rest, or joy or sorrow. It is comforting to know that He who calls us to be holy also grants us the grace to be holy. St. Augustine of Hippo (354–430) understood this important truth when he prayed, "And all my hope is nothing if not in your exceeding great mercy. Give what you command, and command what you will."[2]

## THE MOTIVATION TO BE HOLY

Second, from our text, we learn of the motivation to be holy. God says, "Be holy, for I am holy." Notice that God does not say, "Be holy as I am holy." We are to be holy because He is holy. Our motivation to be holy is the holiness of God. God says, "For I am God, and not man, the Holy One in your midst" (Hos. 11:9). God is the Holy One, for He is incomparably, incomprehensibly, and immeasurably pure, majestic, and righteous (Is. 40:25). He is "glorious in holiness, Fearful in praises, doing wonders" (Ex. 15:11).

The seraphim in heaven circle the throne of God crying to one another, "Holy, holy, holy is the Lord of hosts" (Is. 6:3). The fact that the word "holy" is mentioned three times in a row conveys the overarching nature and luminance of God's holiness. God is so holy that it is not possible for us to encounter God or contemplate His holiness without confronting our own vileness and depravity. When the prophet Isaiah saw the Lord sitting on a throne, high and lifted up, he was traumatized by the consciousness of his own sinfulness and cried out in despair:

> Woe is me, for I am undone!
> Because I am a man of unclean lips,
> And I dwell in the midst of a
> people of unclean lips;
> For my eyes have seen the King,
> The Lord of hosts. Is. 6:5

We should also be motivated to be holy because we are God's own special people (1 Pet. 2:9). God said to the Israelites, "And you shall be holy to Me, for I the Lord am holy, and have separated you from the peoples, that you should be Mine" (Lev. 20:26). God commanded the Israelites

---

2. Augustine, *The Confessions* (Toronto, Alfred A. Knopf, 2001), 239.

to be holy because they were separated from the rest of the nations to be His own special treasure (Deut. 7:6).

We are a chosen generation, a holy nation, and His own special people set apart to proclaim His greatness (1 Pet. 2:9). God does not say, "Be holy as I am holy." None of us can be holy in this life in the way God is holy. But as the children (*teknon*) of God born of the Spirit (John 3:5) and sons (*huios*) of God led by the Spirit (Rom. 8:14), we can reflect the character of our heavenly Father in our conduct. Just as a biological son might increasingly exhibit his father's features as he grows older, we are to reflect God's righteousness, moral purity, and goodness in our actions and attitudes as we mature in the faith.

God's desire is that we become more and more like Christ until we become like Christ in holiness at His revelation. The apostle John wrote, "Beloved, now we are children of God; and it has not yet been revealed what we shall be, but we know that when He is revealed, we shall be like Him, for we shall see Him as He is" (1 John 3:2).

## THE MEANS TO BE HOLY

Finally, we learn from our text of the means to be holy. The Israelites were exhorted to be holy because they were delivered from Egypt by God. The Israelites needed to be redeemed first from their slavery in Egypt before they could be instructed to be holy. Egypt symbolizes bondage and slavery to sin. Similarly, we are summoned to be holy because we have been redeemed from the bondage of sin by the precious blood of Jesus Christ (1 Pet. 1:18). Horatius Bonar (1808–1889) put it well: "The divine order then is first pardon, then holiness; first peace with God, and then conformity to the image of that God with Whom we have been brought to be at peace"[3] The Bible says, "But now

---

3. Horatius Bonar, *God's Way of Holiness* (Pensacola: Chapel Library, Kindle Edition), 52.

having been set free from sin, and having become slaves of God, you have your fruit to holiness, and the end, everlasting life" (Rom. 6:22).

The Israelites of old were called to be a counter-culture, wholly separated unto God, and to be a light to the nations (Is. 42:6; 49:6). But they followed the ways of the ungodly idolaters that surrounded them and became like them. The Israelites failed to meet the holiness requirement of God, because their relationship to God was transactional, instead of being a relationship based on love and a transformed life. The gospel was preached to them, but it did not profit them because they did not respond to it in faith (Heb. 4:2). God's holy law told the Israelites what to do, but it could not give them the power to do it. As a result, the law of God became a yoke of burden that they could not bear (Acts 15:10).

Being holy in an unholy world is not possible without a new heart. Without a new heart, we may externally observe the law, but our heart is far from God. Only Christ can give us a new heart. The Bible says, "Therefore, if anyone is in Christ, he is a new creation; old things have passed away; behold, all things have become new" (2 Cor. 5:17). When the law of God is written on our hearts by the Holy Spirit, we will want to keep His commandments, not because of coercion or compulsion, but because we delight to do the will of God even as Christ delighted to do His will (Jer. 31:3; 2 Cor. 3:3; Ps. 40:7–8). We relate to the law of God differently in that we seek to keep it—not as a legal transaction, but as an expression of our love for God born out of a new heart and a new spirit (Ezek. 18:30–31).

The Bible says that we are sanctified in Christ Jesus and called to be saints (1 Cor. 1:2). This is our positional holiness in Christ. Our positional holiness must be translated progressively into practical holiness in our daily conduct. This happens by our union with Christ. Practical holiness becomes a living reality when we recognize that we have died with Christ, and that sin no longer has dominion over us because of Christ's resurrection from the dead (Rom. 6:6–8). In

Christ, we become partakers of the divine nature and escape the world's corruption caused by human desires (2 Pet. 1:4).

Our union with Christ and identification with His death and resurrection give us the power to put to death the sinful and earthly things lurking within us and to express the fruit of holiness in every area of our lives (Col. 3:5). The Bible says, "For as many as are led by the Spirit of God, these are sons of God" (Rom. 5:14). This is not a statement about the general guidance of the Holy Spirit in a believer's life, but a reference to the enablement of the Holy Spirit "to put to death the deeds of the body" mentioned in Rom. 8:13. We bear the fruit of holiness in our conduct when we die to self. We progress in our sanctification when we daily present our bodies as a living and holy sacrifice to God, which is a pleasing act of worship unto Him (Rom. 12:1).

We have a mandate to be holy and to walk the highway of holiness. We are called to be holy because God is holy. Our motivation to be holy is His holiness. The means to be holy is our union with Christ. In Christ alone we are given a new life and all the resources necessary for life and godliness (1 Pet. 1:3; 1 John 3:6). May the Lord lead us and empower us to be holy, for He is holy.

## PRAYER

*Dear Lord, help me to walk the path of holiness in total dependence on You. Search my heart and know my thoughts. See if there are any wicked ways in me, and lead me in the way everlasting. Let me reflect Your character and let Your grace flow through me. Amen.*

# Living Epistles

> Do we begin again to commend ourselves? Or do we need,
> as some others, epistles of commendation to you or letters
> of commendation from you?
>
> You are our epistles written in our hearts, known and read
> by all men; clearly you are an epistle of Christ, ministered
> by us, written not with ink but by the Spirit of the living
> God, not on tablets of stone but on tablets of flesh, that is,
> of the heart.
>
> — 2 Corinthians 3:1–3

Several years ago, Kouzes and Posner surveyed 75,000 people around the world over a period of 20 years to find out what people expect of their leaders. Their survey showed that, more than anything else, people expect character and principled behavior from their leaders.[1] In other words, people want their leaders to be authentic and "walk the talk." Long before modern research brought this important

1. Kouzes and Posner, *Leadership Challenge* (San Francisco: Jossey-Bass Publishers, 2002) 44.

leadership trait to light, the apostle Paul practiced it. He said to the Christians in Thessalonica, "For when we brought you the Good News, it was not only with words but also with power...And you know of our concern for you from the way we lived when we were with you" (1 Thess. 1:5 NLT). Paul knew the importance of connecting his verbal proclamation of the gospel to his visible actions. Today, many Christians fail in their witness for Christ because they don't connect their voices to their actions.

In the text before us, Paul reminds us that we are the living epistles of Christ seen and read by all people. He wrote to the Christians at Corinth that he didn't have to bring them a letter of commendation from others or ask them to write one on his behalf. Instead, he wrote, "You are our epistle written in our hearts, known and read by all men" (2 Cor. 3:2). Paul was confident that the life lived by the Corinthian believers spoke louder than any letter of recommendation he could have produced concerning his ministry. They were the living epistles bearing witness to the transforming work of Christ.

## OUR LIFE IS AN OPEN BOOK

Three important truths are worth noting in this text. First, we are the living epistles sent by Christ. Paul wrote, "You are a letter from Christ" (2 Cor. 3:3 NLT). We are not our own, for we belong to Christ. He, the author of our salvation, sends us into the world to be the living epistles of the gospel of salvation. Jesus said, "You didn't choose me. I chose you. I appointed you to go and produce lasting fruit" (John 15:16 NLT). Are you living your life in a way worthy of your call? Do others see in you the fruit worthy of your repentance?

Second, we are the living epistles written by the Spirit of God. We read: "Clearly you are an epistle of Christ, ministered by us, written not with ink but by the Spirit of the living God, not on tablets of stone but on tablets of flesh, that is, of the heart" (2 Cor. 3:3). The law of God written on tablets of stone on Mount Sinai was God's will for His people. It told the Israelites what to do but could not help them do it. It killed hope, for no one could keep the law. The Bible calls the law written on tablets of stone the "law of sin and death," because it shows that we are sinners worthy of death (Rom. 8:2).

But the law that is written on our hearts by the Spirit is called the law of the Spirit of life in Christ Jesus, because it not only tells us what to do but also gives us the strength to do it. When the Spirit of God comes into our hearts, He changes us so that we obey the commandments of God because we want to. The motivation to keep the law of God springs from a changed heart, not out of some external obligation. As living epistles, we proclaim the gospel of salvation through a transformed life, which expresses itself in good works (Eph. 2:10).

Third, we are the living epistles read by all people. Whether we realize it or not, we are either authenticating or discrediting the gospel by the way we live. The story is told of four Bible scholars who were arguing over the best Bible translation. One said that he preferred the King James Version because it's written in beautiful and majestic English. Another said he liked the American Standard Bible for its literalism and closeness to the original languages. The third said one of the modern translations is better because it's easy to read and reflects the way we speak.

After listening thoughtfully for a while, the fourth pastor said, "I personally prefer my mother's translation." Surprised by his remark, one of the other pastors said, "We didn't know that your mother is a Bible translator." To which he replied, "Yes sir, she is a translator. She translates every page of the Bible into her daily life, and it's the most convincing translation that I have ever read." That's what it means to be a living epistle!

We must translate the message of Christ in our life. The apostle Paul wrote to the Christians in Thessalonica: "For our gospel did not come to you in word only, but also in power, and in the Holy Spirit and in much assurance, as you know what kind of men we were among you for your sake" (1 Thess. 1:5). Paul was a living epistle to the Christians in Thessalonica.

Do people see Christ in you? Or is the message of Christ obscured by your conduct? Let's not forget that we are called to be living epistles to be read by all.

## PRAYER

*Lord, let my life be a living testimony to Your faithfulness. Let those who come in contact with me see the beauty of Jesus in me. Shine through me, love through me, and touch through me. Amen.*

## DAY 26

# Arise and Shine

Arise, shine;
For your light has come!
And the glory of the Lord is risen upon you.

—Isaiah 60:1–3

Therefore He says:
"Awake, you who sleep,
Arise from the dead,
And Christ will give you light."

—Ephesians 5:14

These passages of Scripture ought to encourage anyone who is in a state of despair or helplessness. If you feel as if you have outlived your usefulness or you don't see a bright future on the horizon, these words of the Lord are for you. In Chapter 60, the prophet Isaiah heralded the dawning of a new day for Israel and trumpeted the future glory of Zion during the millennial kingdom when the splendor and glory of God upon Israel would draw the nations of the world to her.

Today, Israel is like an estranged wife (Is. 50:1), but when the Redeemer returns, she will be cleansed and restored to be a delight to His heart. Isaiah used a literary method called the prophetic perfect tense to speak of the future millennial glory of Jerusalem as though it had already taken place. Moreover, under the inspiration of the Holy Spirit, he foretold the return of the exiles from their Babylonian captivity almost 150 years before the event. He was so certain about the fulfillment of his prophetic word that he spoke to his contemporaries as though the return from exile had already taken place and the exiles were within earshot. By pointing to the future glory of Israel, Isaiah sought to encourage the exiles who would return from Babylon.

Can we apply this word of encouragement to our lives? Absolutely! The key to applying it without doing violence to the text is to understand the significance of the expression, "For your light has come." Isaiah's prophetic announcement must have struck a responsive chord with his hearers, for the Jews had been in pursuit of the light that would enlighten and lift them out of darkness. Looking down the corridor of time, Isaiah said:

> The people who walked in darkness
> Have seen a great light;
> Those who dwelt in the land
> of the shadow of death,
> Upon them a light has shined. Is. 9:2

The "light" foretold by the prophet invaded human history seven hundred years later in the person of Jesus Christ (Matt. 4:16; Luke 1:76–79). Jesus identified Himself as that light when He said, "I have come as a light into the world, that whoever believes in me should not abide in darkness" (John 12:46). Indeed, the light came two thousand years ago to lift us out of darkness. The apostle Paul wrote, "For it is the God who commanded light to shine out of darkness, who has shone in our hearts to give the light of the knowledge of the glory of God in the face of Jesus Christ" (2 Cor. 4:6).

In His incarnate state, Jesus Christ was the face of the light, knowledge, and glory of God. We who live in the present period of salvation history can look back at Christ's first coming and His redemptive work on the cross as God's means to lift us from darkness and hopelessness. To reject Christ, therefore, is to live in darkness. The Bible says, "And this is the condemnation, that the light has come into the world, and men loved darkness rather than light, because their deeds were evil" (John 3:19). There is no excuse to live in darkness, for the light of God has come!

## CALLED TO ARISE

Our text is a clarion call from God for action. First, we are called to rise because our light has come. The word "arise" (*qumi*) is an imperative, a command, and it literally means to stand up or to rise up. The basic meaning of this verb has the idea of someone rising up from a couch or standing up after falling. It also has the idea of living or coming to life again (*qum hyh*). The apostle Paul echoed this theme in his letter to the Christians at Ephesus when he quoted a first-century baptismal hymn based on Isaiah 60:1: "Awake, you who sleep, arise from the dead (*anasta*), and Christ will give you light" (Eph. 5:14).

How can a dead person arise by himself or herself? This is simply not possible without the help of an external agent. Therefore, the command to arise was accompanied by the promise of divine strength to fulfill the command. A better way of translating the text would be, "Arise and shine because your light has come!" St. Augustine, the fourth-century church father, understood the indispensability of divine enablement if we are to carry out God's command. He prayed, "O God, command what you wouldst, and grant what thou dost command."[1]

---

1. R. C. Sproul, "The Pelagian Captivity of the Church," http://www.bible-researcher.com/sproul1.html (accessed December 3, 2016)

We cannot simply pull ourselves by our bootstraps and stand up on our own. Arising from our deadness is not a matter of positive thinking or making some positive affirmations. Jesus had to tell Lazarus to "come forth" before he could arise from the dead. Unless God grants us, we cannot carry out what He commands us to do. Jesus said, "Without me you can do nothing" (John 15:5).

This prophetic word was meant to encourage the exiles that returned to Jerusalem in 536 BC. Jerusalem was in ruins. But the prophet pointed them to the glorious future of Jerusalem as if it had already taken place and commanded them to arise and shine. We too can arise from our darkness and deadness to see the dawning of a new day in our life because of Christ, who said, "I am the light of the world. He who follows me shall not walk in darkness, but have the light of life" (John 8:12).

## CALLED TO SHINE

We are called to shine because our light has come. The Hebrew word *owr*, translated as "shine," means to become light or to be illuminated or enlightened. The light we shine is not an innate light we possess; it is a reflected light. We reflect the light that is given to us. Jesus Christ is the "true light that gives light to every man" (John 1:9).

As the moon reflects the light of the sun in the dark sky, we reflect the light of the Son of God. Paul wrote, "For you were once darkness, but now you are light in the Lord. Walk as children of light" (Eph. 5:8). We are light in the Lord, not in and of ourselves. As children of light, we reflect the glory (*kabowd*, meaning weight, splendor, dignity, and honor) of the Lord because He has risen upon us. Our salvation is a manifestation of God's glory upon us.

What does it mean to shine in a dark world? Jesus said, "Let your light so shine before men, that they may see your good works and glorify your Father in heaven" (Matt. 5:16). We shine and reflect the glory of God when we engage in good (*kalos*) works—works that are pure, honorable, excellent, and so distinguished as to be pleasing in the sight of God—so that everyone will praise our heavenly Father. The light within us enables us to walk as children of light, producing only what is good, right, and true (Eph. 5:9). To shine also means to be able to determine what pleases the Lord and not take part in the worthless deeds of evil around us; instead, we are to expose them (Eph. 5:11).

Florence Nightingale, the founder of modern nursing, was born the daughter of a wealthy English family. Very early in life, she felt called by God to serve others in a very tangible way and chose to become a nurse. During the Crimean War, she went to the battlefield with 38 nurses. The hospital on the battlefield was dirty, but she managed to have the men clean up the place for the care of the wounded soldiers. During the night, she would visit each ward with a lamp in her hand to check how the wounded soldiers were doing, and so was affectionately called the "lady with the lamp."

Literally and figuratively Florence Nightingale was a shining light in a place of darkness, pain, and death. The soldiers called her a ministering angel. The divine light within her enabled her to shine as a light upon a hilltop, giving light in a place of darkness.

## ARISE AND SHINE

Arise and shine. That is the command of the Lord. The good news is that He who calls us to arise and shine also gives us the grace to fulfill His command. Yes, this evil age is all exile for the people of God, but for those who are in Christ, the age to come is a glorious age filled with justice, peace, and righteousness. While we wait for the return of Jesus Christ and the future glory of the millennial kingdom on earth, we need not be disheartened by the darkness— ignorance, evil, sorrow, and destruction—that surrounds us today.

Though Satan has blinded the minds of those who do not believe the gospel, we can live in the light because our light [Jesus Christ] has come "to give light to those who sit in darkness and the shadow of death, to guide our feet into the way of peace" (Luke 1:79). Because we have the light of Christ in us, we are the light of the world and a shining city set on a hill that cannot be hidden (Matt. 5:14). We must let our light shine in such a way that people will see our good works and give glory to our Father in heaven (Matt. 5:16).

## PRAYER

*Lord, let Your light shine through me so that those around may see Your glory and be drawn to You. Empower me to be the light of the world and the salt of the earth. Help me to live in Your light and do works that please You. In Jesus' name, I pray. Amen.*

# Being Blessed in an Unhappy World

> Blessed is the man
> Who walks not in the counsel of the ungodly,
> Nor stands in the path of sinners,
> Nor sits in the seat of the scornful;
>
> But his delight is in the law of the Lord,
> And in His law he meditates day and night.
>
> He shall be like a tree
> Planted by the rivers of water,
> That brings forth its fruit in its season,
> Whose leaf also shall not wither;
> And whatever he does shall prosper.
>
> — Psalm 1:1–6

Some time ago, *U.S. News & World Report* carried a cover story entitled, "50 Ways to Improve Life in 2007." On the top of the list was "Get happy." We all want to be happy. People in every walk of life are seeking happiness. Thomas Jefferson wrote in the Declaration of Independence that the pursuit of happiness is one of our "inalienable rights." Yet, if there is one thing that seems to mark the mood of our times, it is unhappiness. People are unhappy with their families, jobs, relationships, and just about everything that touches their lives.

In a survey done by the Pew Research Foundation in 2006, 15% of respondents said that they consider themselves "not too happy." The rest said they are "very happy" (34%) or "pretty happy" (50%).[1] The problem with such surveys lies in the definition of happiness. For most people, happiness is nothing more than a psychological feeling experienced when one's desires or wants are met. Mortimer Adler, one of the most distinguished philosophers of the twentieth century, said that to define happiness in terms of feeling is a philosophical mistake. He said happiness is much deeper than that; it consists in the moral and ethical quality of a life lived. Only after a person has lived out his or her life can one say whether or not that person was a happy person. In this sense, happiness is not a feeling we experience at any given moment, but a state of becoming.

The Bible calls such a person "blessed." In Psalm 1, the psalmist describes the life of a blessed person, not in terms of psychological feelings that are evanescent, but in terms of the moral and ethical quality of such a life.

## THE PATH OF A BLESSED PERSON

First, we learn that the path of a blessed person is holiness.

> Blessed is the man
> Who walks not in the counsel of the ungodly,
> Nor stands in the path of sinners,
> Nor sits in the seat of the scornful. Ps. 1:1

---

1. Pew Research Social & Demographic Trends, "Are we Happy?" http://www.pewsocialtrends.org/2006/02/13/are-we-happy-yet/ (accessed December 3, 2016).

Blessed are those who depart from a life of sin and turn toward God. Notice the three actions—walking, standing, and sitting—associated with such people. They don't stroll according to the counsel of the ungodly. They don't give heed to their schemes and plans. Second, they don't stand in the path of sinners. In other words, they don't follow their lifestyle. The conduct of the sinners is abhorrent to those who follow the path of holiness. Third, they don't sit in the seat of the scornful. People who are blessed in the sight of God do not assemble with the wicked and participate in their scornful and silly talk. They don't follow the advice of the wicked nor linger with them.

Holiness is not a popular word in our culture, nor is it rightly understood by many in our society. But the fact remains that we are called to a life of holiness or separation from the ways of the world (1 Pet. 1:15–16). The path to holiness begins at Calvary where God made Christ, who never sinned, to be the offering for our sin so that we might become the righteousness of God in Him (2 Cor. 5:21). In Christ, we have all that we need to live a holy life, for in Christ we are partakers of the divine nature (2 Pet. 1:3–4).

## THE PURSUIT OF A BLESSED PERSON

Second, we learn that the pursuit of a blessed person is godliness. "But they delight in the law of the Lord, meditating on it day and night" (Ps. 1:2 NLT). Blessed are those who don't pursue happiness as an end-goal, but who instead pursue God as their chief end. The apostle Paul wrote, "Godliness with contentment is great gain" (1 Tim. 6:6). He admonished Timothy to "exercise godliness," which is "profitable for all things, having promise of the life that now is and of that which is to come" (1 Tim. 4:8). A blessed person delights in the law of the Lord and is devoted to His word. He delights in the law of the Lord because in it he meets with God who alone can give him joy and happiness.

The psalmist says, "The commandments of the Lord are right, bringing joy to the heart. The commandments of the

Lord are clear, giving insight for living" (Ps. 19:8 NLT). In His word, we meet with God. Jesus said, "You search the Scripture, for in them you think you have eternal life; and these are they which testify of Me" (John 5:39). If you have Jesus in your heart, you are most blessed and joyful even in your difficulties. You can rejoice always, no matter what your circumstances are. Leo Tolstoy, the famous Russian writer, said, "To know God and to live is the same thing. God is life."[2] Without God, you live with an existential vacuum that nothing in this life can fill.

## THE PROSPERITY OF A BLESSED PERSON

Third, we learn that the prosperity of a blessed person is fruitfulness.

> He shall be like a tree
> Planted by the rivers of water,
> That brings forth its fruit in its season,
> Whose leaf also shall not wither;
> And whatever he does shall prosper. Ps. 1:3

Today, many think of prosperity only in terms of material blessings. Although prosperity may include material provisions for our life, the psalmist describes prosperity in terms of vitality, productivity, and imperishability. First, blessed people are like a tree planted by the rivers of water. That is, they are full of vitality and life. People who are blessed of God are endowed with the life of God in Christ. Jesus said, "I have come that they may have life, and that they may have it more abundantly" (John 10:10). The "life" that is mentioned in this text is *zoe* or God life.

Second, blessed people are like a tree planted by the rivers of water that brings forth its fruit in season. In other words, people who are blessed are productive in their lives. That is,

---

2. AZ Quotes, "Leo Tolstoy Quotes About God," http://www.azquotes.com/author/14706-Leo_Tolstoy/tag/god (accessed June 6, 2018).

they are known for their fruitfulness. Fruitfulness in this text refers to "good works," which flow out of their life in Christ. Fruitfulness is a characteristic of those who glorify God by being a blessing to others through the exercise of their God-given spiritual gifts. Unfortunately, many are barren in their lives. They have received the word of the Lord joyfully, but because they have no deep roots, they remain unfruitful.

The key to fruitfulness is to abide in Christ. Jesus said, "Abide in Me, and I in you. As the branch cannot bear fruit of itself, unless it abides in the vine, neither can you, unless you abide in Me" (John 15:4). The season for fruit-bearing in your life will begin only when you abide in Christ. God wants you to be productive and a blessing to others. Are you a blessing to those around you for the glory of God?

Third, people who are blessed are like a tree "Whose leaf also shall not wither." Contrast this blessing with the destiny of the ungodly people who are destined to perish (Ps. 1:6). The prosperity of the blessed people is characterized by their imperishability. They have everlasting life while the wicked perish and turn into ashes. Jesus said, "He who believes in the Son has everlasting life; and he who does not believe the Son shall not see life, but the wrath of God abides on him" (John 3:36).

Is it possible to live a blessed life in an unhappy world? Yes, absolutely. The path to such enduring blessedness is a life set apart for God, a life in pursuit of God, and a life that is a blessing to others by the power of God.

## PRAYER

*Lord Jesus, thank You for our work of redemption on the cross of Calvary so that I may experience true joy and peace in a word riddled with sin and strife. Amen.*

## DAY 28

# Desiring God

Whom have I in heaven but You?
And there is none upon earth that I desire besides You.

My flesh and my heart fail;
But God is the strength of my heart and my portion
forever.

— Psalm 73:25–26

What is the "one thing" you desire above any other thing in life? This may be a difficult question to answer, since you may have several things of high priority in your mind that you want to do or experience. In Psalm 73:25, the psalmist tells us what he desired the most in the world. He wrote, "Whom have I in heaven but You? And there is none upon earth that I desire besides You." Simply stated, he wanted God more than anything else in life. Heaven and earth without God are nothing but vast wastelands.

The psalmist sought to live a clean and a righteous life, yet he faced trouble at every turn. He saw the wicked scoff at God and be boastful, violent, and oppressive, yet they lived a life of ease and prosperity. He laments saying, "Did I keep my heart pure for nothing? Did I keep myself innocent for no reason? I get nothing but trouble all day long; every morning brings me pain" (Ps. 73:13–14 NLT). He tried to solve this mystery and inner conflict by the force of reason, but he found it to be an impossible task until he entered the sanctuary of God. In the presence of God, he discovered God's goodness and His justice, along with the ultimate destiny of the wicked. He emerged from this struggle with a longing for God: "There is none upon earth that I desire besides You" (Ps. 73:25).

## THE CHIEF END OF MAN

Do you desire God more than anything on earth? Do you derive your delight and satisfaction from knowing God and experiencing His goodness? Or do you look for your fulfillment and satisfaction in more money, more power, more knowledge, more pleasure, more friends, or in more of any other thing that the world offers? Trying to find satisfaction and fulfillment outside of God is like digging cracked cisterns that can hold no water (Jer. 2:13). Yet this is exactly what many do—forsake the fountain of living water and dig for themselves broken cisterns.

After Paul encountered Jesus on the road to Damascus, he realized that knowing Christ infinitely surpassed anything that the world offered. He said, "I count all things loss for the excellence of the knowledge of Christ" (Phil. 3:8). Malcolm Muggeridge, the British journalist who experienced his share of fame and success, admitted the futility of them all after he found Christ (or, rather, was found by Christ) in his later years. He wrote:

> I may, I suppose, regard myself, or pass for being, as a relatively successful man. People occasionally stare at me in the streets–that's fame. I can fairly easily earn enough to qualify for admission to the higher slopes of the Internal Revenue–that's success. Furnished with money and a little fame even the elderly, if they care to, may partake of

trendy diversions– that's pleasure. It might happen once in a while that something I said or wrote was sufficiently heeded for me to persuade myself that it represented a serious impact on our time–that's fulfillment. Yet I say to you—and I beg you to believe me—multiply these tiny triumphs by a million, add them all together, and they are nothing—less than nothing, a positive impediment— measured against one draught of living water Christ offers to the spiritually thirsty, irrespective of who or what they are."[1]

*The Westminster Shorter Catechism* insightfully states that the chief end of man is to "glorify God and enjoy him forever."[2] Seek your satisfaction in Christ alone. Pursue God by engaging in such spiritual disciplines as worship, prayer, study, and Christian service. Spend more time with the Lord and bask in His presence. When you consciously seek God, you are sure to face distractions that try to keep you from desiring Him. The antidote is to "bring every thought [distraction] into captivity to the obedience of Christ" (2 Cor. 10:5). Make Christ the supreme object of your desire, love, and enjoyment.

## PRAYER

*Lord, there is none on earth that I desire but You. Grant me, by Your grace, the opportunity to know You a little more this year. Amen.*

---

1. Malcolm Muggeridge, *Seeing Through the Eye* (San Francisco: Ignatius Press, 2005), 97.

2. G. I. Williamson, *The Westminster Shorter Catechism*, Second Edition (Phillipsburg: PR Publishing, 1970), 1.

# Be Thankful Always

So Jesus answered and said, "Were there not ten cleansed? But where are the nine? Were there not any found who returned to give glory to God except this foreigner?"

— Luke 17:17–18

In everything give thanks; for this is the will of God in Christ Jesus for you.

— 1 Thessalonians 5:18

Two angels were sent out from heaven, so the story goes, to bring back the prayers and thanksgivings of the people on earth. The Angel of Thanksgiving went with a large hamper to collect the thanksgivings of the people. The Angel of petition went out with a basket to collect the petitions. The Angel of Petition returned with petitions that overflowed the basket and filled a sack as well. The Angel of thanksgiving had only three thanksgivings in his large hamper.

The truth is that most of us are eager to bombard heaven with our petitions for material blessings and God's favor for living a prosperous life. Yet when we do receive God's blessings, too often we forget to thank Him and express our feelings of gratitude. "Gratitude is not only the greatest of virtues," said the Roman philosopher and statesman Marcus Tullius Cicero, "but the parent of all the others."[1]

In Luke Chapter 17, we read about Jesus and His disciples on their way to Jerusalem. When they came to an unnamed village in the region between Samaria and Galilee, ten lepers saw Jesus from a distance. These lepers had been living in small huts outside the village, estranged from the general population. When they saw Jesus, they cried out to Him, "Jesus, master, have mercy on us."

Jesus looked at the lepers, signaled them to be quiet, and said, "Go and show yourselves to the priests." He did not touch them or say to them "be clean." Nor did He tell them to go and dip themselves seven times in the Jordan River. He simply said, "Go and show yourselves to the priests." Why? In those days, only the priests in Jerusalem had the authority to diagnose a leper and certify him as unclean. Conversely, only the priests were authorized to declare a leper who has been healed as clean. So, having commanded the lepers to show themselves to the priests, Jesus went on His way.

Imagine the mental anguish these lepers must have felt at that moment. Jesus had told them to show themselves to the priests even though the lepers had not yet been healed. It would have been more reasonable if Jesus had healed the lepers and then instructed them to go to the priests, as He had done with the leper in Luke Chapter 5. As these lepers looked at their bodies, they saw no signs of healing. The blotches were still there and nothing had changed. I can imagine the lepers saying to themselves: "Is this a joke? Should we go to the priests in Jerusalem or return to our homes in humiliation and discouragement?" Their faith was on trial.

---

1. Brainy Quote, https://www.brainyquote.com/quotes/quotes/m/marcustull122152.html/ (accessed December 3, 2016).

The lepers decided to go anyway and see the priests despite an absence of any visible signs of healing. But as they were going, one of them shouted, "Hey guys, I can't believe it! My leprosy is gone...I am clean." Soon, another echoed his astonishment at the healing he had received. Before long, one after the other began to shout with joy for the healing he had received. While nine of them continued on their journey to see the priests, one of them, a Samaritan, decided to turn around and return to Jesus to express his gratitude.

Isn't it interesting that this Samaritan was in the company of nine Jewish lepers? Though the Jews had no dealings with the Samaritans, he was accepted by these Jewish lepers because, I suppose, misery loves company. They were too miserable to get hung up on their prejudices. In any event, this Samaritan leper decided to return to Jesus and thank Him for what He had done. With a loud voice, he glorified God and prostrated himself before Jesus in gratitude. Jesus looked at the people around Him and said, "Didn't I heal ten lepers? Where are the other nine? Why is it that no one else has come back and glorified God except this foreigner?" With great delight, Jesus turned to the Samaritan and said, "Go your way; your faith has made you well."

## THE SUPPRESSION OF THANKSGIVING

Why was it that none of the nine Jewish lepers return to thank Jesus? Your guess is as good as mine. Maybe they were too eager to go to the priests and be certified as clean. Perhaps they were so excited about their new lease on life that they forgot all about thanking God. A plausible explanation is that these Jewish lepers, as members of the covenant community, felt entitled to the healing they had received from Jesus. They had been told that when the Messiah came He would give sight to the blind, cleanse the lepers, raise the dead, heal the deaf, and cause the lame to walk (Luke 7:19–22). So they probably thought that if Jesus was the Messiah, as foretold by the ancient prophets, He was only doing what He was supposed to do and they were receiving what they were entitled to as members of the covenant community.

It is interesting to note what Jesus asked hypothetically in Luke 17:7–10: would a master say to his servants, when they return from the field, "Come and sit with me and dine"? No! He would say to them, "Prepare my meal. After I eat my meal, you can eat your meal." Does the master thank the servants for doing only what they were supposed to do? Of course not.

Here we have the first principle of thanksgiving: thanksgiving is suppressed when we believe we are entitled to what we have received from God. For example, have you ever considered sending a letter thanking your employer for your monthly or weekly paycheck? The chances are you have not! Why? Because you feel that your paycheck is something that you are entitled to receive for the work done. Aldous Huxley, the author of *Brave New World*, said, "Most human beings have an almost infinite capacity for taking things for granted."[2] If truth be told, even in our redeemed state, we tend to approach God with an attitude that God is a cosmic bellhop at our beck and call to render us service that we are entitled to. Such an attitude of entitlement in any relationship will suppress genuine thanksgiving.

## THE PROMOTION OF THANKSGIVING

In this story, Jesus asked the people: "Why is it that not one of the lepers has come to glorify God except this foreigner?" It must have been quite humiliating to the Samaritan to be called a "foreigner" but the Jews in that day regarded Samaritans as outside the pale of Israel and had no dealings with them. In fact, this Samaritan would not have been able

---

2. Brainy Quote, "Aldous Huxley Quotes," https://www.brainyquote.com/quotes/aldous_huxley_163415 (accessed May 15, 2018).

to go to the temple in Jerusalem and show himself to a Jewish priest. He probably would have had to go to a Samaritan priest to be certified as clean.

The Samaritan leper returned to Jesus because he was overwhelmed with gratitude for what Jesus had done for him. Jesus healed him even though he was not a part of the "people of God." Christ extended His grace to him though he belonged to a different race. The Samaritan's sense of unworthiness for what he had received from Christ caused him to return to Jesus and thank Him. Here we have the second principle of thanksgiving: thanksgiving is promoted when we believe we are unworthy of what we have received from God.

In Luke Chapter 7, we read about a prostitute who came to Jesus with an expensive fragrance while He was in the home of a Pharisee named Simon. She knelt at the feet of Jesus and began to clean His feet with her tears and wipe them with her hair. She kept on kissing His feet and putting perfume on them. The people who were with Jesus were indignant: why would He allow this sinful woman to touch Him? Then Jesus told Simon a parable of two debtors whose debts were canceled by a lender. One owed 500 pieces of silver and the other 50 pieces. Jesus asked Simon, who do you suppose loved the lender the most? Simon answered the one who owed 500 pieces of silver. Then Jesus turned to the woman and said to Simon, "I tell you, her sins—and they are many—have been forgiven, so she has shown me much love" (Luke 7:47, NLT).

Leprosy can serve as a metaphor for the disease of sin from the standpoint of its effects. Just as leprosy separates a person from society and causes the sufferer to be shunned, sin separates us from God and His fellowship. Because of sin, we were once without Christ, being aliens from the commonwealth of Israel and strangers to the promised covenant, having no hope and without God in the world. But we have been brought near to God by the blood of Christ; therefore, we are no longer strangers and foreigners, but fellow citizens with the saints and members of the household of God (Eph. 2:12–19). If we truly understand and grasp this truth, we would fall before God and lavishly thank Him.

## THE APPROBATION OF THANKSGIVING

We read that the Samaritan returned to Jesus and glorified God with a loud voice and fell down on his face at Jesus' feet, giving thanks to Him. While the other nine lepers went to see the priests to be declared clean and offer a series of required blood sacrifices over a period of eight days, the Samaritan returned to Jesus, whose priesthood is superior to the Aaronic priesthood, and offered a sacrifice that is superior to any blood sacrifice. Christ was so pleased by the Samaritan's thanksgiving that He commended him for his faith. Here we have the third principle of thanksgiving: thanksgiving is always accepted by God as a pleasing sacrifice unto Him.

> I will praise the name of God with a song,
> And will magnify Him with thanksgiving.
> This also shall please the Lord better than an ox or bull,
> Which has horns and hooves. Ps. 69:30–31

> Therefore by Him let us continually offer the sacrifice of praise to God, that is, the fruit of our lips, giving thanks to His name. Heb. 13:15

The nine Jewish lepers believed in Christ for their healing, but once they received the healing, they moved on with their lives. The Samaritan also believed in Jesus, but when he received his healing, he was drawn to Christ. He saw Christ as more than a healer. He saw Him as one who was worthy of his worship, adoration, and surrender.

Jesus was so delighted by the Samaritan's thanksgiving that He praised him saying, "Arise, go your way. Your faith has made you well." The Greek word translated as "well" literally means "saved." Jesus gave the Samaritan a revelation, which was denied to the others, that by faith in Christ he not only received healing for his body but also the forgiveness of his sins. He also revealed to the Samaritan the wideness of God's grace, which is not limited to Jews but also extends to Gentiles.

The apostle Paul wrote, "In everything give thanks; for this is the will of God in Christ Jesus for you" (1 Thess. 5:18). Such an unconditional and unceasing thanksgiving is not natural to us; it requires the aid of the Holy Spirit. Paul exhorted the Christians at Ephesus: "Do not be drunk with wine, in which is dissipation; but be filled with the Spirit…giving thanks always for all things to God" (Eph. 5:18, 20). When we cultivate the virtue of giving thanks in every situation, thanksgiving becomes more than a verbal expression; it defines who we are in Christ.

It's been said that Saint Felix of Cantalice, a sixteenth-century illiterate street preacher and friend of the poor, always said *Deo Gratias* ("thanks be to God") when he received something from anyone for his monastery. Soon the people on the street began to call him "Brother Deo Gratias," which became his nickname. Let us likewise resolve to be thankful to God in every situation, for this will please the Lord more than any sacrifice we may offer to Him. *Deo Gratias.*

## PRAYER

*Lord, give me a heart of thanksgiving in every situation that I face in life. Help me to remember that, though a particular circumstance may be unpleasant, You are at work in my life. So teach me to give You praise and thanks in every situation. Amen.*

# Glorification

For whom He foreknew, He also predestined to be conformed to the image of His Son, that He might be the firstborn among many brethren. Moreover whom He predestined, these He also called; whom He called, these He also justified; and whom He justified, these He also glorified.

—Romans 8:29–30

If the church could be aroused to a deeper sense of the glory that awaits her, she would enter with a warmer spirit into the struggles that are before her.

—J. H. Thornwell

# Jesus is Coming Soon

And behold, I am coming quickly, and My reward is with Me, to give to every one according to his work. I am the Alpha and the Omega, the Beginning and the End, the First and the Last. Blessed are those who do His commandments, that they may have the right to the tree of life, and may enter through the gates into the city...And the Spirit and the bride say, "Come!" And let him who hears say, "Come!" And let him who thirsts come. Whoever desires, let him take the water of life freely.

—Revelation 22:12–14, 17

The second coming of Jesus Christ will be the most dramatic and apocalyptic event that the world will ever witness. For those who are not in Christ, it will be a time of unprecedented terror, distress, and loss. But to those who are in Christ and are living in anticipation of His coming, it is a time of glorification; it is a time of being changed from mortality to immortality; from corruption to incorruption. The Bible calls this coming event the blessed hope of a Christian (Titus 2:13). The Bible teaches that all of creation is earnestly longing for redemption from death and decay.

Yes, Jesus is coming again. The Old Testament prophets predicted the return of the Messiah. The apostles preached about the coming of Christ. Peter and Paul expressly wrote about the coming of Christ. But most of all, Jesus Himself assured us of His coming. In Job, the oldest book in the Bible, we read:

> For I know that my Redeemer lives,
> And He shall stand at last on the earth;
> And after my skin is destroyed, this I know,
> That in my flesh I shall see God. Job 19:25

In the text before us, the apostle John quotes the words of Christ, which he heard in a vision while he was incarcerated on the island of Patmos. He was there not because of any crime he committed, but because of the word of God and for the testimony of Jesus Christ. As John's vision came to a conclusion, Jesus said these final words: "And behold, I am coming quickly, and my reward is with Me, to give to every one according to his work. I am the Alpha and the Omega, the beginning and the end, the First and the Last" (Rev. 22:12–13). From this text, we learn three important truths about the coming of Christ.

## THE PROMISE OF HIS COMING

First, we learn of the promise of Jesus's return. "And behold, I am coming," said Jesus. There was a sense of urgency in His tone. There was a sense of certainty in His promise. In John 14, Jesus made this promise to His distressed and discouraged disciples: "Let not your hearts be troubled; you believe in God, believe also in Me. In my Father's house are many mansions; if it were not so, I would have told you. I go to prepare a place for you. And if I go to prepare a place for you, I will come again and receive you to Myself that where I am, there you may be also" (John 14:1–3).

After Jesus made that promise, He went to the cross to pay the penalty for our sins. He died and was buried in a borrowed tomb. On the third day, He rose triumphantly from the grave for our justification. After His resurrection, He appeared to His disciples and others on ten separate occasions over a period of forty days. Then, while His disciples watched Him, He was taken up into heaven. As they looked steadfastly toward heaven, two men stood by them in white garments and said: "Men of Galilee, why do you stand gazing up into heaven? This same Jesus, who was taken up from you into heaven, will so come in like manner as you saw Him go into heaven" (Acts 1:11). Indeed, Jesus is coming again. The next big event on His calendar is His return to earth.

In 1989, a terrible earthquake took place in Armenia. It lasted only four minutes, but the result was utterly devastating. Thirty thousand people died in that earthquake. Soon after the tremors stopped, a father rushed to the nearby school to find his son. When he reached the site, he found the school reduced to a heap of rubble. The whole building was flattened. As he stood there, he remembered what he had promised his son. He said, "Son, no matter what happens, I'll be there for you." With tears in his eyes, the father located the boy's classroom. He started removing one stone after another.

People came to help, but soon they told him, "It is no use. All the children are dead." But the Father would not give up. He and his friends removed stones for hours. Soon, 16 hours went by, then 32 hours, and then 38 hours. He came across a huge stone, and with the help of others, he moved it. Behind the stone, in a hole, was his son. When the father heard his son's voice, he cried out, "Arman, Arman!" The boy responded, "Here I am dad, here I am dad!" Then the boy said these heart-warming words: "Dad, I knew you would come for me. I told the boys that if you are alive you would come for me and save me and the rest of the boys. I told them you promised, 'No matter what happens, I will be there for you.'" That's the power of a promise.

If an earthly father could keep his promise, how much more shall our Lord keep His word? Jesus said, "Heaven and earth will pass away, but My words will by no means pass away" (Matt. 24:35). Jesus will keep His word because He is alive. Are you ready to meet your God? He is coming soon to reign as the King of Kings and Lord of Lords.

## THE PERIOD OF HIS COMING

Second, we learn of the period of Jesus's return. Jesus said, "Behold I am coming quickly." He is coming quickly. Over the years many people have speculated about the timing of His return, but they all have been wrong. Some have written books and profited for themselves. But they have been put to shame. Jesus said: "But of that day and hour no one knows, neither the angels in heaven, nor the Son, but only the Father" (Mark 13:32).

While we don't know the exact time or the hour of Jesus' coming, we know the manner in which He is coming. First, He is coming unexpectedly. To illustrate the point, Jesus said, "As the days of Noah were, so also will the coming of the Son of Man be" (Luke 17:26). In the days of Noah, people were carrying on with their lives as usual—eating and drinking, marrying and giving in marriage. They did not know that disaster had struck them until the flood came. The flood caught them unaware. Noah warned his generation for nearly 120 years, but they scoffed and ridiculed him. Jesus said that just as the flood came upon them when they were least expecting, so will the coming of the Son of Man be at an hour when we do not expect Him. The apostle Paul wrote that the day of the Lord comes as a thief in the night (1 Thess. 5:2).

Second, Jesus is coming suddenly. He said, "As the lightning comes from the east and flashes to the west, so will the coming of the Son of Man be" (Matt. 24:27). The Bible says when people are saying everything is peaceful and safe, then disaster will fall on them as labor pains come upon a woman with child (1 Thess. 5:3). Third, He is coming loudly. The Bible says He is coming with the voice of the archangel and with the trumpet of God (1 Thess. 4:16).

The apostle Paul wrote that Christ will return at the last trumpet with a loud noise (1 Cor. 15:52). And when the last trumpet is blown, all of heaven will be saying, "The kingdoms of this world have become the kingdoms of our Lord and of His Christ, and He shall reign forever and ever" (Rev. 11:15). Jesus said that He will send His angels with a great sound of the trumpet, and they will gather His elect from the four corners of the earth (Matt. 24:31).

Fourth, Jesus is coming gloriously. Jesus said, "For the Son of Man will come in the glory of His Father with His angels" (Matt. 16:27). He is coming in triumph and power. Once He came to suffer, but now He is coming to reign. Once He came in humiliation, but now He is coming in glory. Once He came as a servant, but now He is coming with authority and power to rule the world.

Jesus said to watch and be ready for His coming. Watch for what? We must watch for the signs of His coming. What are some of the signs? There will be a widespread apostasy and turning away from God (1 Tim. 4:1). People will be giving themselves to demonic activities and occult practices. The Bible says that in the last days, people will increasingly become lovers of themselves and of money, boasters, blasphemers, disobedient to parents, proud, unholy, unthankful, without self-control, unforgiving, headstrong, and lovers of pleasures rather than lovers of God. They will have a form of godliness but no power (2 Tim. 3:1–5).

There will be widespread persecution of believers. We are already seeing that in many parts of the world. It will only grow in intensity. Even in countries where there is relative freedom, persecution will come. There will be an increase in knowledge at a lightning speed. We are witnessing that right now. Technological advances in knowledge generation, storage, retrieval, and transmission are staggering. Jesus spoke of cosmic upheavals that will occur before His return. People will go from place to place seeking peace, but instead will find intense distress.

But in the midst of these terrible signs, there is one important sign with a high note of optimism. The Bible says that the gospel of the kingdom shall be preached in the entire world as a witness to all peoples, and then the end will come (Matt. 24:14). There are over 14,000 ethnic groups in the world today, and evangelistic efforts are being intensified to reach these groups.

What should we do? We need to be ready. Are you ready to meet Him? The Bible says that when Noah was warned about the coming flood, he was moved with fear and built the ark. If you are moved with a holy fear, you will seek to enter into the ark, which is Jesus Christ. Only He can save you from the coming destruction.

## THE PURPOSE OF HIS COMING

Finally, we learn of the purpose of Jesus's return. Jesus said, "Behold, I am coming quickly, and my reward is with Me, to give to every one according to his work" (Rev. 22:1). He is coming to settle all accounts and reward everyone according to his or her work. The Bible says that each one of us will stand before Him to give an account of our life—every word, every thought, and every action. The Bible says God has appointed a day to judge the world in righteousness by that Man whom He has ordained He has given assurance of this by raising Jesus Christ from the dead (Acts 17:31).

When General Douglas MacArthur was forced to leave the Philippines during World War II, he told the Filipinos: "I shall return." He kept his promise and returned to the Philippines in victory. After he returned, he made another speech saying, "I have returned." The first speech would have been worthless without the second, which gave it force and meaning. So Jesus promised to return to give every one according to his work, and He will return to keep His promise.

Our reward will be to enter into His joy and reign with Him. "Blessed are those who do His commandments that they may have the right to the tree of life, and may enter through the gates into the city" (Rev. 22:14). Inside the city of God, there will be no more tears, no more pain, no more sorrow, no crying, and no more death. We will be with the Lord forever.

Are you looking forward to the return of Jesus Christ? Dean Farrar was a personal friend of Queen Victoria. On the occasion of the first anniversary of the accession of Edward VII to the throne of England, he related the story of Queen Victoria, who had heard one of her chaplains preach at Windsor on the second coming of Christ. After telling Dean about it, she said, "Oh, how I wish that the Lord would come during my lifetime." "Why does your Majesty feel this very earnest desire?" asked Dean Farrar. With her countenance illuminated with deep emotion, she replied, "Because I should so love to lay my crown at His feet."[1] Indeed, the day is coming soon when every knee shall bow and every tongue shall confess that Jesus Christ is Lord.

## PRAYER

*Lord, grant me Your grace to live with the blessed hope of Your imminent return. Help me to purify myself just as You are pure and look forward to Your glorious return. Amen.*

---

1. Walter Knight, *Master Book of New Illustrations* (Grand Rapids: Eerdmans Publishing Company, 1956), 605.

## DAY 31

# One Thing I Do

Brethren, I do not count myself to have apprehended; but
one thing I do, forgetting those things which are behind
and reaching forward to those things which are ahead, I
press toward the goal for the prize of the upward call of
God in Christ Jesus.

— Philippians 3:13–14

The month of January is named after the Roman god
Janus, who symbolizes new beginnings. Interestingly, he
is depicted as a two-faced god, each face looking in the
opposite direction. One face is frowning, symbolizing the
past, while the other face is smiling, pointing to a bright
future. As we make the journey of life, let us put behind us
our past regrets, disappointments, failures, accolades,
successes, and triumphs and forge ahead with confidence that
our best days are yet to come.

As Christians, how then must we live in the present
moment? The apostle Paul gives us a strategy for living that is
based on the premise that "existence follows essence." How
we live is determined by our essential relationship with God

through Christ. He says God's desire for us is that we fulfill the purpose for which Christ Jesus has laid hold of us. For everyone who is saved by grace through faith, that purpose is to become more like Christ. Paul regarded his life as a race toward Christ-likeness. But he was honest enough to admit that though he was saved and secure in Christ, he had not become all that God wanted him to be. He saw himself as God's work in progress.

Paul gives us three action steps that we can take in the present moment to move toward the goal that Christ Jesus has set out for us.

## FORGET

First, we must forget what is behind us. Just as a foot racer dares not look back, we must not look at what is behind us. By this Paul does not mean that we must erase the memory of the past. Aristotle said, "Memory is the scribe of the soul."[1] We need memory to recall the past goodness of God and to commune with our hearts. What Paul means is that we consciously refuse to allow our past laurels, failures, regrets, and disappointments to impede our progress. They are of no value in running the race of life. Jesus said, "No one, having put his hand to the plow, and looking back, is fit for the kingdom of God" (Luke 9:62 ).

When we fail to forget our past, the devil uses our past to bring us under condemnation and causes us to miss what the Lord is doing in the present moment. We can confidently relinquish our checkered past because we have a new "past" in Christ. He bore our past upon Himself on the cross so that everyone who is in Christ is given a new past. The Bible says, "Therefore, if anyone is in Christ, he is a new creation; old

---

1. Philosophy Paradise, "Famous Aristotle quotes," http://www.philosophyparadise.com/quotes/aristotle.html (accessed December 3, 2016).

things have passed away; behold, all things have become new" (2 Cor. 5:17). Only God in Christ can change our past.

## FOCUS

Second, we must focus on what is before us. Paul says we must concentrate on what is in front of us to move toward the mark. An actor who made an indelible impression on me for his dramatic prowess and versatility is the legendary Omar Sharif, best known for his roles in *Lawrence of Arabia* and *Doctor Zhivago*. During an interview, he was asked, "What do you see in the next couple of years for yourself?" Without missing a beat, Sharif replied:

> Ask me what I see in the next couple of hours…that's all. I believe, when you are young, you should think of the future. When you are old, you should not think of the future and you should not think of the past. You should concentrate on the moment you are living because you don't know how long you have. And you can't waste time remembering things. I don't remember anything. I don't want to remember…All the films I made are nothing to me. They have disappeared from my mind. I think of what I am doing now.[2]

Omar Sharif's existential view of life is sensible to the extent that a slavish preoccupation with our past is of no value. In fact, it is detrimental. What is important is the present moment. But where Omar Sharif and other existentialists like him err is in relegating the significance of our present moment only to mere temporal existence, with no consideration for the eternal consequences of what we do in the present moment.

What was Paul's goal during his earthly life? It was Jesus— to gain a full and complete knowledge of Jesus Christ.

---

2. YouTube, "Omar Sharif on acting, religion, and the future," https://www.youtube.com/watch?v=KpxoknyYydI&start_radio= 1&list=RDQMfm1DYBNDxtA (accessed May 8, 2018).

Though he knew that his knowledge of Christ on this side of resurrection would remain partial, he was determined to press forward to know Him more and more. He knew that he must await the return of the Lord and the future eternal state when "that which is in part will be done away" (1 Cor. 13:10) and when we see God face to face (Rev. 22:4).

We too must seize the challenges, opportunities, trials, and divine appointments that come to us each day and forge ahead toward the goal of knowing Christ and increasing our knowledge of God (Col. 1:9–12). This requires an intense desire and an earnest effort on our part. But that is not enough. We need the aid of the Holy Spirit, whose task is to help us comprehend "what is the width and length and depth and height—to know the love of Christ which passes knowledge, that [we] may be filled with all the fullness of God" (Eph. 3:18–19).

## FORESEE

Third, we must foresee the prize beyond us. Paul says, "I press toward the goal for the prize of the upward call of God in Christ Jesus" (Phil. 3:14). No athlete would participate in a contest if there is no reward to be won. The Bible says, "Do you not know that those who run in a race all run, but one receives the prize? Run in such a way that you may obtain it" (1 Cor. 9:24). The prize that Paul refers to is the divine approbation we receive from God when we complete the race. The imagery drawn in this text from Greek games is the commendation received by the athlete from the umpire, who announced the winner's name, his father's name, and the name of his country. He would then give the winner a palm branch as his prize.

Paul says our prize is our "upward call of God," when Christ Himself commends us, saying, "Well done, good and faithful servant" (Matt. 25:21). And our prize is the imperishable crown, which is the full revelation of Jesus Christ and the transformation of our body that it may conform to Christ's glorious body (Phil. 3:20–21; 1 John 3:2).

Thomas Chalmers said: "Mathematician that I was, I had forgotten two magnitudes—I thought not of the littleness of time—I recklessly thought not of the greatness of eternity."[3] In the light of eternity, let us not expend our time on that which is impermanent. Instead, let us run our race by relinquishing our past, seizing the present, and pursuing the prize of God in Christ Jesus.

## PRAYER

*Dear Lord, let today be the day of new beginnings for me. Help me to forget what is behind and focus on the goal of being more like Christ. Grant me the grace to see the prize of the upward call of God in Christ Jesus and live my days faithfully so I may receive it. Amen.*

---

3. William Hanna, *Memoirs of the Life and Writings of Thomas Chalmers*, vol. 3 (New York: Harper & Brothers, Publishers, 1857), 89.

# About the Author

Abraham Philip is the founder and president of Proclamation Ministries and travels as an evangelist and conference speaker. He retired from DuPont after twenty-two years of service, where he held research and managerial positions. He holds a BS in biology from Pacific Lutheran University in Tacoma, Washington, and an MS in microbiology from Eastern Michigan University in Ypsilanti, Michigan. In addition, he earned an MA in religion from Liberty University in Lynchburg, Virginia, and a PhD in pulpit communication from Trinity Theological Seminary in Newburg, Indiana.

In 2016, the Olford Center in Memphis, Tennessee, conferred on Abraham the title of Stephen Olford Fellow of Expository Preaching. He and his wife, Annie, have three grown children and two grandchildren. They make their home in Newark, Delaware.

## Contact Information

Proclamation Ministries
P.O. Box 9700
Newark, DE 19714

www.proclamationministries.org
Email: info@proclamationministries.org

23155240R00112

Made in the USA
Columbia, SC
06 August 2018